Text copyright © The Consultative Group on Ministry among Children 2010
Illustrations copyright © Peter Stephenson 2006
The authors assert the moral right
to be identified as the authors of this work

Published by
The Bible Reading Fellowship
15 The Chambers, Vineyard
Abingdon OX14 3FE
United Kingdom
Tel: +44 (0)1865 319700
Email: enquiries@brf.org.uk
Website: www.brf.org.uk
BRF is a Registered Charity

ISBN 978 1 84101 700 6

First published 2010
10 9 8 7 6 5 4 3 2 1 0

Acknowledgments
Unless otherwise stated, scripture quotations are taken from the Contemporary English
Version of the Bible published by HarperCollins Publishers, copyright © 1991, 1992, 1995
American Bible Society.

Scripture quotations taken from the Holy Bible, New International Version, copyright © 1973,
1978, 1984 by International Bible Society, are used by permission of Hodder & Stoughton
Publishers, a member of the Hachette Livre UK Group. All rights reserved. 'NIV' is a
registered trademark of International Bible Society. UK trademark number 1448790.

Scripture quotations taken from The New Revised Standard Version of the Bible, Anglicized
Edition, copyright © 1989, 1995 by the Division of Christian Education of the National
Council of the Churches of Christ in the USA, are used by permission. All rights reserved.

Scripture quotations from *The Message*. Copyright © by Eugene H. Peterson 1993, 1994, 1995.
Used by permission of NavPress Publishing.

A catalogue record for this book is available from the British Library

Printed in Singapore by Craft Print International Ltd

More Core Skills

FOR CHILDREN'S WORK

Extended learning skills for church-based children's ministry

The Consultative Group on Ministry among Children

Core Skills for Children's Work is offered as extended training material by the Consultative Group of Ministry among Children (CGMC), a network of Churches Together in Britain and Ireland.

Churches and organisations currently represented on CGMC

Baptist Union of Great Britain
Bible Reading Fellowship
Children Matter
Children's Ministry
Christian Education
Christian Education Association of Scotland
Church of England
Church of Ireland
Church of Scotland
Church in Wales
Church Lads' and Church Girls' Brigade
Congregational Federation
Council for Sunday Schools and Christian Education in Wales
CTBI
Episcopal Church of Scotland
Girls Brigade
Godly Play UK
Methodist Church in Britain
Methodist Church of Ireland
Moravian Church in Great Britain and Ireland
Presbyterian Church of Wales
Presbyterian Church in Ireland
Quaker Life
Roman Catholic Church
Roots for Churches
Salvation Army
Scripture Union
Sunday School Society of Ireland
United Reformed Church
Welsh National Centre for Religious Education
World Council of Churches

Acknowledgment

CGMC wishes to thank all those involved with the project, either with the writing or the field-testing of material, and is grateful for their ideas, inspiration and hard work, which have enabled the development of this additional training material.

Particular thanks go to Karen Bulley and Mary Hawes for acting as coordinators for the project, to Doug Swanney for guiding the initial steps, and to the many CORE Skills groups who have used the original CORE material and encouraged the publication of these further six modules.

We also extend a special thank you to the Westhill Endowment for their generous support for the writing, launching and ongoing development of the CORE project.

From the writing group

Core Skills for Children's Work and *More Core Skills for Children's Work* were written by members of the ecumenical Consultative Group on Ministry among Children (CGMC).

CGMC was constituted in its present form in 1972 and is an official network of Churches Together in Britain and Ireland (CTBI). It exists to bring together all those with national responsibility for work with children in denominations and Christian agencies that are in sympathy with the aims and objectives of Churches Together in Britain and Ireland. It has initiated research and specific projects relating to children's ministry, leading to publications and reports which have been shared with the different denominations.

CGMC members meet in conference twice a year, when specific issues relating to children's ministry are discussed in depth. At each CGMC conference, a business meeting of all member bodies is held. This is the decision-making body of the organisation and it elects an executive committee with a moderator, secretary and treasurer. CGMC is self-financing, being funded by membership fees from its members.

From time to time, CGMC has also organised larger conferences, bringing together a wide group of regional children's workers and, more recently, has organised CORE conferences for trainers.

CGMC has a long history of publishing works that have had a profound influence on the understanding of children in the Church. This tradition continues to the present day with new ecumenical training material for workers in the form of *CORE Skills*. Previous and current works include:

- *The Child in the Church*: A ground-breaking report on the Church's need for children and the child's place within the Church, published in 1984 by the British Council of Churches.

- *Children and Holy Communion*: A thought-provoking review of theory and practice in different denominations, published in 1989 by the British Council of Churches.

- *Kaleidoscope*: A popular training programme for children's leaders, exploring both theory and practice, published in 1994 by Christian Education. A Welsh edition was also produced, supported by CGMC.

- *Taking Care*: A pack produced by the National Children's Bureau with contributions from CGMC to provide training for leaders who have to relate to issues of child abuse.

- *Big Blue Planet*: A selection of songs for children to share with adults, published by Stainer and Bell in 1995.

- *Unfinished Business*: A report from 2000 encouraging churches to move forward with their ministry among children, published by Church Council of Britain and Ireland.

- *Tuesday's Child*: A reader for Christian educators, published by Christian Education in 2001.

- *Core Skills for Children's Work*: Training material for all those working in children's ministry, written by CGMC and published by Barnabas in 2006.

- *More Core Skills for Children's Work*: Additional training material for all those working in children's ministry, written by CGMC and published by Barnabas in 2010.

CGMC is also a participant in the European Conference on Christian Education (ECCE), a forum for churches and agencies to discuss children's ministry (Protestant, Catholic and Orthodox) across Europe. This triennial conference considers major thinking related to Christian education in general and work with children in particular. In recent years the conference has convened in Estonia, Czech Republic, Italy, Belgium, Austria and France.

More about the work and membership of CGMC can be found on its website at www.cgmcontheweb.com

Important information

Photocopying permission

The right to photocopy material in *More Core Skills for Children's Work* is granted for the pages that contain the photocopying clause: 'Reproduced with permission from *More Core Skills for Children's Work* published by Barnabas 2010 (978 1 84101 700 6)', so long as reproduction is for use in a teaching situation by the original purchaser. The right to photocopy material is not granted for anyone other than the original purchaser without written permission from BRF.

The Copyright Licensing Agency (CLA)

If you are resident in the UK and you have a photocopying licence with the Copyright Licensing Agency (CLA), please check the terms of your licence. If your photocopying request falls within the terms of your licence, you may proceed without seeking further permission. If your request exceeds the terms of your CLA licence, please contact the CLA directly with your request. Copyright Licensing Agency, 90 Tottenham Court Rd, London W1T 4LP. Tel 020 7631 5555; fax 020 7631 5500; email cla@cla.co.uk; web www.cla.co.uk. The CLA will provide photocopying authorisation and royalty fee information on behalf of BRF.

BRF is a Registered Charity (No. 233280)

Contents

Foreword

Down to earth, accessible training for people engaged in working with children is an essential. The original *Core Skills for Children's Work* materials have proved enormously valuable for thousands already. This fresh volume is a great addition to the CORE family.

If I have a small apple to eat and I decide to take a large bite out of it all at once, there is every likelihood that I will find myself biting into a tough chewy bit at the core. I may even find an apple pip in my mouth (OK, so I've got a large mouth). Such a bite can make the whole eating experience less pleasurable; the tough bits in the middle are rather less palatable than the sweet surrounding flesh. When any of us work with children, it is not long before we discover aspects of the work that are tougher to handle—even, less sweet. It is some of these issues, in one sense, that these new varied materials seek to tackle. Each session is helpfully framed with worship. Each has plenty of options for how to tackle the issues concerned. There is plenty of relevant information alongside opportunities to explore the issues from people's own experience.

Unlike the apple core, however, which never becomes less tough than or as sweet as the main flesh, the reality is that these tough issues may prove to become very sweet. Taking a global perspective, helping children to be advocates and developing them as young leaders all add whole new dimensions to working with young people. Transitional times and challenging behaviour can be real opportunities for growth and development; working with special needs can be extraordinarily rewarding.

A further important aspect of these materials is that they have been produced by those who are passionate about working together across denominational and theological boundaries, for the good of the church's work with children. In doing so, they demonstrate the value of training being done in a similar way on the ground. These sessions could be run by a church working on its own, but they would be more rewarding if done by people from different churches learning together.

One final thought: working with children can be hard work; it can be tough and challenging. It is also very rewarding and enjoyable. There is every reason why training should be enjoyable too: we tend to learn better that way. So bite into these materials and enjoy the sweet taste they offer.

+Paul Butler
Bishop of Southwell and Nottingham

Introduction

Guiding principles

All children are made in the image of God. They are loved unconditionally by God and were affirmed in the life and ministry of Jesus. This is reflected in the Christian community, where:

* God's love is made real through human life and relationships.
* All children and adults are of equal value.
* The Holy Spirit speaks powerfully through children as well as adults.
* Everyone experiences enjoyment, safety and encouragement in belonging.
* All contribute and all receive, learning from each other.
* The Bible is accessible to all.
* All respect one another as people of faith.
* Differences are acknowledged and diversity celebrated.
* All are being changed by the love of Christ and share the good news in the wider community.
* Worship, celebration and encountering God are vital to the growth of faith.
* All have a sense of belonging to the universal Church and of serving the world together.

Rights of the Child

The UN Convention on the Rights of the Child has been an important document for all those working with children, both in and out of the Church. Its main drives are reflected through CORE, and are as follows.

* Calling for the provision of specific resources, skills and contributions necessary to ensure the survival and development of children to their maximum capability.
* Requiring the creation of means to protect children from neglect, exploitation and abuse.
* When adults are making decisions that affect children, children have the right to say what they think should happen and have their opinions taken into account, while recognising that the level of a child's participation in decisions must be appropriate to the child's level of maturity.

Safeguarding and Child Protection

More CORE Skills for Children's Work does not include Child Protection training. Most denominations in Britain and Ireland have their own policies, procedures and training, to which all participants in *More CORE* should look.

More CORE Skills for Children's Work recognises the centrality of Safeguarding and Child Protection to all our work with children, so we recommend that the information sheet on page 14 is completed by all participants before starting *More CORE*. A copy of this sheet can be included in your portfolio.

CORE aims and learning outcomes

Aim One

To help participants to develop an understanding of children and the skills required to nurture children in their journey of faith.

Learning outcomes

* To experience and understand the process of how people develop, learn and grow in faith.
* To listen to and accompany children as partners in faith.
* To evaluate their own skills, gifts, strengths and weaknesses and identify a plan for personal development.
* To help children engage with the Bible as a part of the living, personal and ongoing story.
* To work creatively with children, using a variety of methods to suit different learning styles.
* To develop skills to encourage children in expressing and valuing their spirituality and making their own response of faith.
* To share resources and ideas.

Aim Two

To provide the participants with the opportunity to explore and reflect on their own experience of faith and Christian journey, and the effect it has on their work with children.

Learning outcomes

✤ To recognise the need to feel valued, equipped and supported in their role.

✤ To reflect on and share their own faith story.

✤ To develop a reflective, enquiring approach to the Bible and its use in faith and life.

✤ To explore their experience of worship, celebration and spiritual life.

✤ To recognise the role of, and raise their awareness of, children's ministry.

✤ To develop the skills and habit of reflecting on their work with children.

Aim Three

To help participants capture and share a vision of a Christian community in which children's faith is expressed and valued.

Learning outcomes

✤ To articulate an understanding of God's call to be a pilgrim people, a missionary community and a global family.

✤ To advocate the active participation of children in mission and ministry.

✤ To explore ways of working with children in a variety of contexts, including new expressions of church.

Using More CORE

This material is planned for ease of use in a variety of ways. As the material has been written from a number of ecumenical settings, it is hoped that it will be delivered ecumenically wherever possible.

If you would like to know where your nearest *More CORE* course is happening, visit the CORE website (www.coreskillsforchurches.com), contact CGMC (www.cgmontheweb.com) or ask your denominational or organisational office.

The basic skills for children's ministry (child development, leadership, programme planning, pastoral awareness, spirituality and the Bible) are covered in *Core Skills for Children's Work*.

The six sessions in *More Core Skills for*

Children's Work are designed as 'stand alone' modules, covering specific issues and building on the basic skills. It is expected that an individual or group will select a module appropriate to their needs and then perhaps cover the remaining modules at a future date.

Each session is designed to take two hours. This timespan will be achieved by selecting from the material available. Each session could be extended to cover a whole day by using more of the material, adding some from the website and slowing the pace in items used, to allow more discussion, exploration and activity. The 'apple indicators' shown beside each activity have been developed to give an idea of how long that item might take.

✤ One apple indicates a simple introductory activity that might take only a short time to complete.

✤ Two apples indicate a more in-depth activity that will require some thought and time.

✤ Three apples indicate a high-content section containing the main thrust of the teaching.

By choosing more of the one-apple activities and fewer of the three-apple ones, you will have a shorter session. The reverse, of course, will give a longer session.

A *More CORE for Children's Work* session is laid out as follows.

✤ **Aim** of the whole module.

✤ **Learning outcomes** that should be achieved through the session.

✤ **Materials needed** to run the session.

✤ **Opening thought** to enable reflection.

✤ **Starters:** ways into the topic.

✤ **More CORE:** the main teaching element.

✤ **Biblical thought:** tying the teaching to the Bible.

✤ **Reflection on learning:** a prompt to help better understanding of the session.

✤ **Worship:** suggestions to close the session in themed worship.

✤ **Personal Reflection sheet** to assist participants in noting their learning outcomes.

✤ **Portfolio checklist** for those wishing to collect evidence of learning.

The CORE website is an exciting part of the training. It offers many additional resources, web links, articles and book suggestions, which will help all participants to expand their CORE knowledge.

Website features include:

* Resource lists for each CORE session (updated and extended regularly).
* A list of courses posted by trainers across the UK and Ireland.
* Contact details for denominations and organisations.
* New CORE modules for sale and download as they are made available.
* Bulletin boards for those involved in CORE and More CORE.
* Resources for trainers, including PowerPoint, logos and certificates.

The Personal Reflection sheet can be completed by the participant at home or at the end of the session. It is intended to enable further thought on the following questions.

* What encouragements, concerns and challenges has this module raised for you?
* What would you like to explore further?
* What action will you take or encourage your church community to take as a result of this module?
* What will be the benefits for the children in your group and for your church community?
* Which aspects of this session can you talk about and check out with the children in your group?

For those who want to use *More CORE Skills for Children's Work* as part of an accredited learning course, the portfolio checklist summarises the learning for which you would need to show proof, in order to satisfy the requirements. More information on *More CORE* and accreditation will be available on the website.

Session Six: Young leaders

Session Six is a training module for existing young leaders or prospective young leaders aged about 14–18, introducing them to the role of a children's worker.

The material and the exercises are designed to be used by a group of young leaders led by two experienced children's workers who have some training competence. However, many of the activities could be used by a mixture of young leaders and the adult leaders with whom they already work. Indeed, this could lead to more insightful discussions about the transition a young leader is experiencing, and a better mutual understanding of what may be reasonably expected from a young leader. If the adult leaders are present, the trainers may need to agree some rules at the outset so that this module primarily benefits the young leaders. For example, in discussions young leaders should be invited to speak first, while adults comment afterwards.

The module can be used on its own or in conjunction with other *CORE Skills* and *More CORE Skills* sessions. Alternatively, young leaders could complete the main *CORE Skills* session and take this module as an extra unit to explore issues particular to their situation.

Weekender

You could use Session Six as the focus of a weekend for young leaders by:

* Extending some of the activities.
* Exploring the 'Top tips' handouts in more detail.
* Combining this session with some of the other *More CORE Skills* sessions.
* Adding some food and social activities.
* Preparing together to lead the worship service at church on Sunday.
* Inviting adult leaders, with whom the young leaders usually work, to attend part of the weekend to explore the expectations placed upon young leaders.

Mentoring

Young leaders are likely to develop their leadership skills more effectively if they have an experienced mentor who can:

* Demonstrate good practice.
* Encourage, reassure and build confidence.
* Help them to reflect on and learn from their experience of leadership and their observations of other leaders.
* Direct them to further training where it might be appropriate.

The simple model below may be a helpful pattern for mentors to follow.

I do, you watch.
We do together.
You do, I watch.

Top tips handouts

The 'Top tips' handouts (pages 122–124) are given to aid young leaders in their practical work with children. They are not intended as comprehensive guides but simply to help young leaders get started.

Safeguarding and Child Protection

Title of your denomination's policy document:

What do you do if you have an issue relating to safeguarding and child protection?

Who is the person in your church who deals with safeguarding and child protection issues?

What permission and registration forms do you complete when a new child joins the group?

What training in safeguarding and child protection have you had?

If none, when is the next available training?

When is the next review of your local safeguarding and child protection procedures?

Reproduced with permission from *More Core Skills for Children's Work* published by BRF 2010 (978 1 84101 700 6) www.barnabasinchurches.org.uk

Introductory session

Aim

To provide a basic introduction to working with children in a church context.

Learning outcomes

❖ To share hopes and fears about working with children.
❖ To reflect critically on a variety of strategies for developing relationships with children.
❖ To evaluate the use of a code of conduct.
❖ To explore issues around children, theology and culture.
❖ To consider how to approach a session with children.
❖ To determine future learning needs.

Materials needed

Before the session

✳ Labels or name badges for people as they arrive

Starters

✳ Flip chart paper and pens
✳ An apple
✳ Post-it notes

Core

✳ Copies of 'Children and church' questionnaire (see page 20)
✳ Copies of 'Assessing training needs' questionnaire (see page 21)

Opening thought

'Are not two sparrows sold for a penny? Yet not one of them will fall to the ground unperceived by your Father. And even the hairs of your head are all counted. So do not be afraid; you are of more value than many sparrows.'
Matthew 10:29–31 (NRSV)

Our role in working among children for the church involves being God's representative in communicating God's love and care. That love and care is also shown to children by the way we act towards each other as adults. In this learning session, the group will not count the hairs on each member's head, but will develop a better understanding of each other's role in children's ministry.

Starters

Who am I?

> You will need:
> ✳ Flip chart paper and pens

In threes, check that you know each other's names, then find out about the context of each other's children's work. Talk about:

❖ How you each feel half an hour before a session begins.

❖ Your hopes and concerns about working with children and young people.

There will be feedback only on the hopes and concerns, which should be written on flip chart paper.

In the whole group, feed back your hopes and concerns and write them on flip chart paper. Then discuss the hopes and concerns that the children may be bringing to the groups with which the participants are involved. Write them up on the flip chart too, and compare this list with the first.

Think about how to find out how children are really feeling. Why is it important to find out?

Apple consequences

> You will need:
> ✳ An apple

Take the apple and start off a story about it: for example, 'This apple came from a small orchard not far from here, and one day…' Pass the apple to someone else in the group, who must continue the story, using the word 'apple' in their contribution to the story. Pass it around the whole group so that everyone contributes, and continue until the story is complete.

Why am I here?

> You will need:
> ✳ A flip chart or large sheet of paper, and pens
> ✳ Post-it notes

How many ways can this question be answered? Write as many as you like, one on each Post-it note. It is up to individuals how they interpret the question. Stick the responses on to a flip chart, without comment.

Join up with one or two other people and talk more specifically about why each person is here in this group. Come back into the whole group and talk about the experiences of this activity.

❖ How did different people interpret the question?

❖ How did people feel during the Post-it exercise?

❖ What insights does this exercise give into working with children?

CORE

Children and their culture

Any adult who wants to work with children needs to understand a little about what it is like to be a child in today's world. The way an adult sees the world is quite different from the way a child sees it. An adult leader can never be a child, but can make some effort to get inside the world of children.

There are many important and powerful influences on children, and the values that are strongly communicated through the media are significant and formative. Spending time on children's websites and reading magazines aimed at children is a good investment and gives pause for thought.

Look at a selection of children's magazines. Skim-read them to get a feel of the impact and tone of the publication. As you read:

❖ Ask yourself what is the message being given there about school/home/lifestyle/spirituality/ young women.

❖ List any words or phrases you don't recognise.

❖ Identify one or two articles that you would like to share with the rest of the group.

❖ Note the main themes of the advertising.

Share your findings with the rest of the group. If there is time together, try putting the values that children observe and experience in the media alongside those communicated explicitly and/or implicitly by the church, and see the differences. Make two lists and ask:

❖ Which culture is easier to understand?

❖ How easy is it to be part of both?

❖ How easy is it to make choices within each culture?

❖ If the church is 'counter cultural', what does that mean?

Children and church

> You will need:
> * Copies of the 'Children and church' questionnaire (see page 20)

Individually, complete the 'Children and church' questionnaire and then share responses together. How far are these statements true of the church you attend? (Mark 0 for 'Not true at all' and 5 for 'This is clearly our church's belief and practice'.)

Approaching a session

Share the experience of a memorable session you have led with children, one you have seen led, or one you experienced as a child. What worked well and why did you remember it?

What challenges have you met, or are you anticipating, in your work with children? Compile a list of these challenges under the following headings:

❖ Starting a session

❖ Using time in a session

❖ Working with a whole group

❖ Choosing activities

❖ Working with other leaders

The following thoughts may start off your discussion.

Starting a session

Think about how the tone is set in the first five minutes (atmosphere, layout, welcome and so on). How can you start the session off to build relationships with the children?

Using time in a session

When planning, always build in time to engage with a group and individual children. Consider the fact that one-to-one conversation is usually easier when a child is engaged in a practical task, especially a low-key task.

Working with a whole group

Use 'circle time' techniques from time to time. With younger children, a 'show and tell' can be an important, regular part of the session. For older children, frequent positive affirmation games will build up the group's capacity to relate positively and share more deeply.

Choosing activities

Always plan to spend time on what is important, and avoid giving time to activities that benefit the adults more than the children. For example, if you meet on a Sunday morning, avoid a weekly commitment to 'producing' something that has to be performed for the adults in church.

Working with other leaders

Consider how you plan and review together.

Assessing training needs

> You will need:
> * Copies of the 'Assessing training needs' questionnaire (see page 21)

This session has drawn attention to just some of the skills and knowledge that are important for any adult working with children on behalf of the church. Some of this skill comes with experience, but only if you take time to do some conscious learning as well, and also take time to reflect critically on your experiences. Look at the outline of the More CORE sessions on the 'Assessing training needs' questionnaire and fill in the boxes to help you assess which topics are priorities for you.

Biblical thought

Children and church

Split into three groups, each group looking at one of these Bible passages: Psalm 78:1–8; Matthew 18: 1–5; Luke 13:34–35.

If this was the only passage in the Bible you read, what would your 'theology' (your understanding of God's view) of children be? Try to sum it up in three statements, and briefly sum up how this would affect the life of the whole church. What do you feel now about the way you would work with children in your church, and why?

In the whole group, consider the different 'theologies' that different church traditions have, and the different ideas there are about why children are in the church. You may recognise the following models.

✤ If the children are considered to be the church of tomorrow and will only become useful disciples when they become adult members, the provision for children may be aimed at keeping them in contact with the church so that their real learning and work can begin when the time comes.

✤ If the children are seen as the church of tomorrow but need to lead a Christian life now, the children's work may be seen as a schooling in the Christian life. The children's activities may work on the assumption that the faith must be learnt and a Christian way of life followed. Information giving and Bible teaching will aim to lead to a vibrant adult faith and spiritual life.

✤ If children are seen as being as much a part of today's church as the rest of the congregation, and equally valuable members, then it will be vital that children's provision in the church is of a high quality, aimed at equipping their ministry. Children will be enabled to take part in all aspects of church life.

If someone came into your church and tried to guess what your theology of children was by watching the life of the church, what conclusions do you think they would draw? Think about visiting another church and guessing what their theology of children might be.

Reflection on learning

Building relationships with children

What is the group's observations of how they have all worked together so far?

Every group has some principles about how the relationships in the group will work—between children, between adults, and between children and adults. Some of those principles will be explicit (having quiet periods to listen to others, keeping each other safe by not running around, and so on) and some implicit (how children address adults, how the children are involved in decision making, and so on)

In a new group, in an established group meeting for the first time after a break, or in a group with lots of new members, it may be good to work together to produce a code of conduct and agree on it. The process for doing this will be important: perhaps there will be some suggestions from both adults and children, followed by a voting procedure to decide

which ones are to be included. Read the following examples and share your responses to them.

Rules set by the leaders
Don't run.
Don't shout.
Don't answer back.
When the leader is talking, listen.
Have fun!

Rules compiled by the children
Welcome to our club. We hope you have a good time, but when you are here you need to do things in our club way. We don't like anyone skittin' people, because we are all friends. Don't bring any sweets or chocolate just for you! We like playing silly games and running round, but when the leaders tell us to stop, we STOP! You'll probably find out that we are all a bit (very!) noisy and talk too much. But we need to remember that when one of the leaders is telling us what to do, we shut up and listen. And we need to listen to each other as well.

We have one word that is banned—BORING. And we don't use any swear words at all. We have drinks every week so you don't need to bring your own. Finally, at the end of the night, no one goes home until someone comes to pick them up.

We hope you have a good time at our club.

Rules agreed by everyone
Be nice.
Help others.
Do the activities when the leaders ask us to.
Make new friends.
Help new people.
Enjoy ourselves.
Listen carefully.
Walk.
Join in.
Don't hit or kick people.
Don't refuse to join in.
Don't be nasty.
Don't run round the room.
Don't talk when someone else is talking.
Don't leave the club room.

How would you go about working with your group to agree a 'code of conduct'?

Worship

Read 1 Corinthians 12:4–6. As a focal point, have a selection of apples used in different ways: apple juice, apple pies, toffee apples and so on. Take time while listening to some music to consider the gifts and talents that you have in relation to children's ministry, because we all have a concern for children and can offer our different skills in different ways. Finish this meditation with a prayer together.

Suggested song

The Lord is good to me
and so I thank the Lord
for giving me the things I need,
the sun and the rain and the apple seed.
The Lord is good to me.

And every seed that grows
will grow into a tree,
and one day soon there will be apples there
for everyone in the world to share.
The Lord is good to me.

'Johnny Appleseed':
http://www.scoutingresources.org.uk/songs/songs_short.html#
johnnyappleseed

At the close of the session, invite everyone to share in the variety of apple products together, in celebration of their involvement in children's ministry.

Children and church questionnaire

Mark **0** for 'Not true at all' and **5** for 'This is clearly our church's belief and practice'.

1.	Children are considered important in our church.	0 1 2 3 4 5
2.	People in our church feel comfortable with children.	0 1 2 3 4 5
3.	Children in our church are happy to be there.	0 1 2 3 4 5
4.	People in our church are willing to support children's work by praying.	0 1 2 3 4 5
5.	People in our church are keen to see children involved in worship throughout the year.	0 1 2 3 4 5
6.	Children are encouraged to join in with other church activities as well as worship.	0 1 2 3 4 5
7.	The adults in our church talk to the children and know their names.	0 1 2 3 4 5
8.	When the children enter the church, they are ignored, but someone greets their parents.	0 1 2 3 4 5
9.	We want children in our church to keep the church going in the future.	0 1 2 3 4 5
10.	There is evidence around the building of the children's involvement in church life.	0 1 2 3 4 5
11.	Our church wants our children to see that God loves them and has a purpose for their lives.	0 1 2 3 4 5
12.	Our church wants children to become active members of the church today.	0 1 2 3 4 5
13.	We want children to be able to look back, later in life, with warm affection at what church meant to them.	0 1 2 3 4 5

Reproduced with permission from *More Core Skills for Children's Work* published by BRF 2010 (978 1 84101 700 6) www.barnabasinchurches.org.uk

Assessing training needs questionnaire

No knowledge: **N**   Some knowledge: **S**   Fully confident: **F**

More CORE Session 1: Transitions

✤ I understand the key transitions in children's lives. ☐

✤ I use active listening skills. ☐

✤ I have strategies for supporting children and their families and carers. ☐

✤ I understand the role of spiritual development in coping with transition. ☐

More CORE Session 2: Special needs

✤ I have an overview of the different needs of children. ☐

✤ I am aware of the issues and difficulties surrounding special needs. ☐

✤ I understand current practice and working environments in special needs. ☐

✤ I know how to enable full participation of children with special needs. ☐

More CORE Session 3: Challenging behaviour

✤ I can define what is meant by disruptive behaviour. ☐

✤ I understand what causes disruptive behaviour. ☐

✤ I am aware of the differing attitudes and behaviours of adults regarding children's behaviour. ☐

✤ I can employ strategies and good practice to help modify children's behaviour. ☐

More CORE Session 4: The global dimension

✤ I understand the ways in which the Christian faith is expressed and experienced around the world. ☐

✤ I am aware of insights from other cultures and perspectives. ☐

✤ I can work with the challenges and complexities of our global faith. ☐

✤ I know how to explore engagement through mission and biblical material. ☐

More CORE Session 5: Children's advocacy

✤ I understand what is meant by advocacy. ☐

✤ I can recognise the attitudes and stumbling blocks that prevent advocacy from taking place. ☐

✤ I understand the role of local schools councils—the child advocate. ☐

✤ I know how to advocate the importance of children's, youth and family work in the church and wider community. ☐

More CORE Session 6: Young leaders

✤ I understand the importance of training young leaders. ☐

✤ I can recognise and confirm the unique contribution that young leaders can make. ☐

✤ I am aware of the range of leadership styles and factors that influence leadership. ☐

✤ I know how to communicate effectively with young leaders. ☐

Reproduced with permission from *More Core Skills for Children's Work* published by BRF 2010 (978 1 84101 700 6) www.barnabasinchurches.org.uk

MORE CORE SESSION ONE
Transitions

Aim

To enable workers to support children through the different transitional experiences in their journey from infancy to early adolescence.

Learning outcomes

❧ To know and understand the key types of transition in the lives of children.
❧ To develop active listening skills and trusting relationships with children.
❧ To develop strategies for supporting children and their families and carers.
❧ To understand the role of spiritual development in coping with transition.

Materials needed

Starters

✳ Circle Line and District Line diagram printed out (one per pair)
(download from www.coreskillsforchurches.com/2367)

Core

✳ 'Transitions and strategies for developing resilience' PowerPoint presentation
(download from www.coreskillsforchurches.com/2367)
✳ Accompanying handouts: 'Transitions' (see pages 26–27) and 'Building resilience'
(see page 28)
✳ 'Attending and listening' PowerPoint presentation
(download from www.coreskillsforchurches.com/2367)
✳ Accompanying handout: 'Attending and listening' (see page 29)
✳ 'Fowler's stages of faith development' PowerPoint presentation
(download from www.coreskillsforchurches.com/2367)
✳ 'Comparative development' handout (A3) printed out (one per person)
(download from www.coreskillsforchurches.com/2367)

Reflection on learning

✳ Personal reflection sheets photocopied from page 30

Worship

✳ Reflective music
✳ Slips of paper and pens or pencils (one per person)
✳ A basket or bin

Opening thought

Adults tend to identify acute and major life events as stressful, whereas children emphasise the primacy of daily hassles, for example, conflict with peers or between parents, or transitional events such as changing schools.
Tony Newman and Sarah Blackburn, 'Transitions in the Lives of Children and Young People: Resilience Factors', *Interchange* 78 (Barnardo's Policy Research and Influencing Unit)

Starters

Life lines

> **You will need:**
> * Circle Line and District Line diagram downloaded and printed out (one per pair)

Consider the Circle Line diagram as an overview of a selection of lifetime key transitional periods. In twos and threes, create a District Line of stations indicating transition events and/or processes affecting children through to early adolescence. As a whole group, compare the diagrams and reflect on the range of stations identified in the small groups.

Discuss the following questions.

* What do we understand by the word 'transition'?
* Can we agree our own definition in the group?

CORE

Input

> **You will need:**
> * 'Transitions and strategies for developing resilience' PowerPoint presentation
> * 'Transitions' handout (pp. 26–27)
> * 'Building resilience' handout (p. 28)

In plenary (that is, the whole group), work through the 'Transitions and strategies for developing resilience' PowerPoint presentation and, as a group, take time to digest everyone's thoughts on the material. Use this exercise as a basis to support input to the rest of the CORE material.

Supporting children in transition

> **You will need:**
> * 'Attending and listening skills' PowerPoint presentation
> * 'Attending and listening' handout (p. 29)

In plenary, work through the 'Attending and listening skills' PowerPoint presentation and take time for everyone to digest the material. Next, get into pairs and ask each pair to choose a sharer and a listener.

Work through the following listening exercise.

* Bring to mind a time in your life when you experienced a transition.
* Share with your partner what happened.
* How did you cope?
* What kind of support did you need?
* Who was around to support you?
* Where was God for you at this time?

Reverse the procedure, so that each person has a chance to be a sharer and a listener.

Spirituality and faith development

> **You will need:**
> * 'Fowler's stages of faith development' PowerPoint presentation
> * 'Comparative development' handout (A3) downloaded and printed out

In plenary, work through the 'Fowler's stages of faith development' PowerPoint presentation and take time for everyone to digest the material. The A3 handout can be used as a separate comparative diagram to place Fowler's and Westerhoff's stages alongside each other and also to give a timeline. The handout can also be used for further study after the session.

As a group, discuss the following question.

* Do faith development models help to identify how transitions impact on children?

Support strategies

In the light of the session so far, in plenary, discuss the implications for leaders in the following areas.

Self-awareness
* How self-aware are you?
* How do you cope with transition?

Activities and programmes
* How do our activities and programmes support children?
* What manageable risks are built in?

Faith and spirituality
* How do faith development models help to identify how transitions impact on children?
* What are the implications for children's spirituality?

The church community

♣ Are significant adults available for the children in our church?

♣ Who are they?

♣ How do they become more accessible?

♣ Is there a sense of significance and solidarity for children in the church?

The wider community

♣ Who else supports the children you work with (at home, school and so on)?

♣ What agencies might you refer to, for support for yourself or the children, if you feel you cannot offer the most appropriate support yourself?

♣ Who else in the community could you work in partnership with?

Biblical thought

A woman's faith _____

Read Mark 7:24–30.

The Syro-Phoenician woman faced a major crisis point in her life with resilience. She would not be put off by Jesus' apparent rebuff. Do you think she would have considered his comment to be racist, sectarian or chauvinistic? How did Jesus deal with the challenge to his reaction to the woman's request? Was this a transition moment for him? Discuss!

Reflection on learning

You will need:
* Personal reflection sheets photocopied from page 30

Using the Personal reflection sheet, draw out action points for yourself in your ongoing work with children.

Worship

You will need:
* Reflective music
* Slips of paper and pens or pencils (one per person)
* A basket or bin

During a time of musical reflection, write down a 'Commitment to action' decision on a slip of paper. Invite everyone to place their slips in a basket or bin, and offer prayers of commitment to working with children.

For the reflective music, use hymns such as 'Jesus, take me as I am' (*Mission Praise* 382) or 'Take my life' (*Mission Praise* 624).

Useful resources

Strong Tower, Kutless, BEC Recordings, Fischy Music (www.fischy.com)

A transition is the change from one state or phase of life to another, or a change in circumstances. Children face many transitions, such as:

✤ Dependence to independence
✤ Immaturity to maturity
✤ Critical events, such as bereavement and separation of parents or from parents
✤ Chronic events, such as long-term illness

Many transitions are 'firsts' for children and can feel daunting. For example:

✤ First day at school
✤ First exam
✤ First girl or boyfriend

Emotional health, well-being and resilience

For J. Bird and L. Gerlach,[1] children need 'good enough' emotional health and well-being to cope with transitions. They will have:

✤ A secure sense of who they are (although this changes over time and develops as they grow).
✤ A sense of being able to be themselves, which is accompanied by aliveness, vitality and energy.
✤ A sense of self-worth that sustains them in the face of setbacks.
✤ A belief in their own ability to influence things and make changes.
✤ An ability to identify, ask for and move towards the things they need.
✤ An ability to recognise, care about and take responsibility for the impact of their behaviour on others.
✤ A willingness and ability to do things with others and/or alone.
✤ A capacity to respect the need for appropriate boundaries for self and others.
✤ A sense of belonging and connection to a few significant people.
✤ A capacity to tolerate uncertainty and respond creatively and with integrity to the challenges life brings.
✤ A way of making sense of their experience to sustain them through life's challenges.

The last three points enable children to manage their risk-taking from a position of strength.

Key skills for managing transition

✤ Manage risk-taking and cope with the outcomes.
✤ Have optimism and a sense of possibility.
✤ Be self-aware and able to learn and develop from experience.
✤ Celebrate success.
✤ Be able to ask for help.
✤ Take care of oneself.
✤ Develop empathy.
✤ Manage loss.

Just as children learn different skills from supervised play and free play, they need both to be able to take risks with and without supervision (as appropriate) and learn from the consequences.

Ali Worthy, 'Supporting children and young people through transition', *Spotlight briefing*, NCB, November 2005

Some principles for supporting effective transitions

✤ Identify key changes, critical moments and transition points for children and young people.
✤ Ensure that your work with children builds life skills, including emotional resilience and empathy, and emphasises the importance of asking for help and support when they are needed.
✤ Identify individuals who may need particular support through transitions. Identify the support mechanisms and agencies that are available for the child and their family. Work in partnership to provide this support where possible.
✤ Involve children in providing support to their peers as part of everyday friendships and relationships.
✤ Involve and support parents and carers in transitions work so that they can celebrate the transitions and provide understanding and support.
✤ Encourage optimism and work with the excitement and opportunities, as well as the fears and anxieties, caused by change and transition.
✤ If the behaviour of a child changes, encourage them to acknowledge it and talk about it. Are there issues relating to transition and change that are causing difficulties, and what can be done to address them?

Reproduced with permission from *More Core Skills for Children's Work* published by BRF 2010 (978 1 84101 700 6) www.barnabasinchurches.org.uk

❖ Provide consistent responses to critical moments and events in children's lives, such as when they are bullied, bereaved or experiencing parental separation. Ensure that the child is at the heart of deciding what support and help they need. Discuss with children when they would be happy for their peers and others to know and understand what has happened, and who they would wish to inform those peers and others.

Notes

1   J. Bird and L. Gerlach, *Improving the Emotional Health and Well-being of Young People in Secure Care: Training for staff in local authority secure children's homes* (National Children's Bureau, 2005)

Reproduced with permission from *More Core Skills for Children's Work* published by BRF 2010 (978 1 84101 700 6) www.barnabasinchurches.org.uk

Building resilience handout

Resilience factors operate in three dimensions, as shown in the table below. The factors listed are those that have a *positive* effect on the child's resilience.

The child	The family	The environment
Active, good-natured temperament	Warm, supportive parents	Supportive extended family
Gender (girls before adolescence / boys during adolescence)	Good parent–child relationships	Successful school experiences
Age (i.e. being younger)	Parental harmony	Friendship networks
Higher IQ	Valued social role (for example, care of siblings)	Valued social role (for example, job, volunteering, helping neighbours)
Social skills	Close relationship with one parent	Close relationship with unrelated mentor
Personal awareness		Membership of religious or faith community
Feelings of empathy		
Self-control		
Humour		
Attractiveness		

When children themselves are asked what helped them 'succeed against the odds', the most frequently mentioned factors are help from members of their extended families, neighbours or informal mentors, and positive peer relationships, rather than the activities of paid professionals.

Strategies for developing resilience

❖ Strong social support networks.
❖ The presence of at least one unconditionally supportive parent or parent substitute.
❖ A committed mentor or other person from outside the family.
❖ Positive school experiences.

❖ A sense of mastery and a belief that one's own efforts can make a difference.
❖ Participation in a range of extra-curricular activities that promote self-esteem.
❖ The capacity to reframe adversities so that the beneficial as well as the damaging effects are recognised.
❖ The ability, or opportunity, to 'make a difference' by helping others or through part-time work.
❖ Not to be excessively sheltered from challenging situations that provide opportunities to develop coping skills.

Newman and Blackburn, 'Transitions in the Lives of Children and Young People: Resilience Factors'

Reproduced with permission from *More Core Skills for Children's Work* published by BRF 2010 (978 1 84101 700 6) www.barnabasinchurches.org.uk

Effective attending tells the other person that you are with them, and puts you in a position to listen.

In his book *The Skilled Helper* (Thomson Learning, 2006), Gerard Egan identifies 'micro-skills' involved in attending. He uses an acronym, SOLER, to help us remember them.

S Face the person Squarely.
O Adopt an Open posture.
L Lean slightly towards the person.
E Maintain good Eye contact.
R Try to Relax.

Skills of listening

✤ **Stop talking**: The focus must be on the other person talking.

✤ **Prepare yourself to listen**: Try to free your mind of other issues.

✤ **Put the talker at ease**: Help the talker to feel free to talk. Think SOLER.

✤ **Remove distractions**: Focus your mind on what is being said. Don't doodle, tap, shuffle papers and so on. Find an appropriate environment, and switch off the phone.

✤ **Empathise**: Show genuine interest.

✤ **Be patient**: A pause, even a long one, does not mean that the person has finished speaking. Be comfortable with periods of silence.

✤ **Listen exactly**: Listen to what the person is really saying, not what you think she or he should be saying.

✤ **Listen to tone of voice**: Tone, volume and pitch can give the listener clues to the person's feelings.

✤ **Listen for ideas, not just words**: You want to get the whole picture. A surface grievance may hide an underlying problem.

✤ **Find out**: Probe gently. Check your own understanding and repeat back what you think you have heard.

✤ **Watch non-verbal communication**: Body posture, gestures, facial expressions and so on are all important. Non-verbal communication can deny or confuse what is being said verbally. It can also confirm what is being said.

Empathic listening

Empathic listening means 'entering the private, perceptual world of the other and becoming thoroughly at home in it. It involves being sensitive, moment by moment, to the changing felt meanings which flow in this other person, to the fear or rage or tenderness or confusion or whatever that he or she is experiencing. It means temporarily living in the other's life, moving about delicately without making judgments'.

Carl Rogers, *A Way of Being* (Houghton Mifflin, 1995)

Personal reflection sheet

What did you learn from this session?

```
```

How will this affect the way you work with children?

```
```

What further items in this area would you like to follow up?

```
```

Reproduced with permission from *More Core Skills for Children's Work* published by BRF 2010 (978 1 84101 700 6) www.barnabasinchurches.org.uk

Portfolio checklist

Learning outcomes

❖ To know and understand the key types of transition in the lives of children.

❖ To develop active listening skills and trusting relationships with children.

❖ To develop strategies for supporting children and their families and carers.

❖ To understand the role of spiritual development in coping with transition.

To show that the learning outcomes have been achieved, your portfolio must include at least the following. *(Tick when you have included each one in the file.)*

☐ Personal reflection sheet

☐ Notes taken during the session, with any additional ideas

☐ Circle Line and District Line diagram with any annotations in the light of discussion and reflection

☐ Reflections on the listening exercise, both as a sharer and as a listener

☐ Notes you have taken based on the exploration of the 'Transitions' PowerPoint presentation

☐ Strategies and support you have identified from reflecting on your children's work situation

☐ Action points identified from the 'Reflection on learning' exercise. Include any action you have taken as a result, and how it has improved your support of the children

The participant's involvement in a group for More CORE Session 1, 'Transitions', is confirmed. The learning outcomes have been achieved through the evidence provided.

Signed (assessor) ———————————————— Date ————————————————

Any comments from assessor

Signed (candidate) ———————————————— Date ————————————————

Reproduced with permission from *More Core Skills for Children's Work* published by BRF 2010 (978 1 84101 700 6) www.barnabasinchurches.org.uk

MORE CORE SESSION TWO
Special needs

Aim

To develop a knowledge and understanding of children with disabilities and explore ways to make all activities accessible, inclusive and welcoming.

Learning outcomes

✤ To gain an overview of some of the different needs people may have.
✤ To develop an awareness of issues and difficulties faced by children with disabilities.
✤ To reflect on current practice and working environments.
✤ To explore ways to enable a child to participate fully in activities.

Opening thought

Across the UK, a child is diagnosed with a severe disability every 25 minutes. Although some children need hospital care, 98% of disabled children live at home with a parent or other family member.
Contact a Family: website www.cafamily.org.uk

Ubuntu is a Swahili concept expressing the belief that 'people are people through other people'. *Namaste*, the traditional Hindi greeting, is thought to have an original meaning of 'I recognize the divine in you'.

What sort of greeting or welcome does the group you run for your children give to different sorts of people? Think about body language and symbolic actions as well as verbal communication. Does the body language match the verbal communication? What sort of welcome does the environment give?

Materials needed

Starters

✱ Paper and pencils
✱ Flip chart

CORE
Gaining an overview of special needs
✱ Handouts describing dyspraxia, Down's Syndrome, autistic spectrum disorder, visual impairment, hearing impairment and celebral palsy (see pages 42–47)

Communication
✱ Paper and pencils

Visual
✱ Blindfolds (one per pair of participants)
✱ Protective goggles or glasses (one pair per participant)
✱ Vaseline
✱ Jigsaw puzzles

* Bread, butter and jam
* Knives and paper plates
* Crayons and scissors
* Simple pictures to colour and cut out

Auditory
* Two cards with the same sentence written on each one
* Earplugs (one pair per pair of participants), or CD player or MP3 player with headphones

Physical
* A wheelchair
* Tape or strips of fabric plaster
* Bandages
* A simple meal
* A craft activity

Dependency
* Thick winter gloves or gardening gloves
* A simple meal (such as cereal and juice)
* Cutlery (such as knives, forks, tablespoons)
* Items of clothing (such as skirts, trousers, shirts, socks, laced shoes)

Attitudes
* Post-it notes with statements written on them

Support and conflict
* Flip chart paper and pens

Information
* Sample consent forms
* Sample information profiles

Worship
* A bunch of flowers
* 'I am special' lists or flower pictures, from 'Starters' (see page 35)

NB: The term 'special needs' (used throughout this module) encompasses all areas of people's needs and ability to participate or engage. The term 'special educational needs' (SEN) focuses on learning, generally in formal educational settings.

Starters

I am special

On a piece of paper, draw five things that are distinctive about you. For each item, describe one or two things that other people can do to enable that attribute to be a positive quality, or to help you make the most of it. How can others help you be the distinctive person God wants you to be?

Discuss this question: 'In what way are the things you have "special needs"?'

Alternatively, give each person a piece of paper and a pencil. Ask them to draw a simple flower on the paper (making the petals big enough to write something in) and write their name in the centre. When everyone has drawn their flower, ask the group to pass the pieces of paper around to one another. Each person then needs to write (in a petal) a quality of the person named in the centre of the flower. When everyone has written something, the flower is returned to the person named.

These qualities are the things that make each one of us special. Each quality will be different, demonstrating that we are individuals. It is sometimes difficult to see positive qualities in ourselves.

NB: Ask people to keep their piece of paper safe, as it will be needed for the time of worship at the end of the session.

What are special needs?

Make a list on the flip chart of things that might constitute 'special needs' in children. Ensure that each person's suggestions are respected and received without the need for justification.

Review the list and summarise it to form a definition of 'special needs' in no more than 15 words, covering all the things that have been suggested.

Practical experience

What special needs do members of the group have experience of…

✤ personally?
✤ in their children's groups?
✤ in their churches?

Share the experiences and your feelings about them.

CORE

Gaining an overview of special needs

See pages 42–47 for a basic description of the following conditions. Please note that these are some of the more common conditions—the list is not exhaustive.

✤ Dyspraxia
✤ Down's Syndrome
✤ Autistic spectrum disorder
✤ Visual impairment
✤ Hearing impairment
✤ Cerebral palsy

The descriptions may be used as handouts during the session or as preparatory reading before the session. These pages also give further contact details for information and advice on these common impairments.

Divide into small groups, each group taking one of the special needs descriptions. Discuss the following questions.

✤ What might be particularly helpful to children with these needs?
✤ What may be unhelpful?
✤ What extra resources would be useful?
✤ What sort of learning activities might be effective?

Alternatively, participants may wish to give a little time to share their experience of particular issues and individual children (while, of course, preserving confidentiality). Think about how these issues might affect you as children's workers or helpers, or as church members in general. Also, think about what the specific needs of the children might be and how they may best be met.

Recognise, as you discuss different needs, that while it is important to gather information, it is equally important to know the individual child and form good relationships with parents or carers, so that you can benefit from the detailed knowledge of the people who know the child best. You may also have the opportunity to talk to other adults you know, in the congregation or elsewhere, who have impairments and who may help you gain more understanding.

Developing awareness of special needs

It is important to think about different impairments and the issues that surround them, and about some of the difficulties that children with special needs, and their families, might encounter. This enables us to recognise how we help or exclude different people.

It is helpful to think, too, about the language we use. While children may have an 'impairment', it is only their environment that may 'disable' them. The terms have been defined by some disabled people in the following ways.

- ❖ **Impairment**: An injury, illness or congenital condition that causes, or is likely to cause, a loss or difference of physiological or psychological function.
- ❖ **Disability**: The loss or limitation of opportunities to take part in society on an equal level with others, due to social and environmental barriers.

'How might you feel if…?' is a helpful question to pose. The exercises that follow are a way to learn a little more about what life may be like with a disability or a particular set of needs.

Choose from the following exercises and activities, enabling people to experience some of the difficulties and so become more aware of them. In pairs after each exercise or activity, reflect generally on the experience. Think about what happened. How did you feel? After the initial reflection, discuss the following questions.

- ❖ How does it feel to need, to trust, to depend or to rely upon others?
- ❖ What were the emotions you experienced?
- ❖ What were the frustrations you experienced?
- ❖ Which is easier, being a helper or being helped?

Communication

Some people have difficulty with verbal communication or find difficulty in receiving and following instructions. Others have impaired understanding of communication. Try this exercise as a way of glimpsing some of the feelings and frustrations involved in what may be an everyday difficulty for many people.

Divide into pairs. Each person needs a pen or pencil and a piece of paper. Each pair sits back to back and decides who will draw and who will give instructions. The person giving instructions draws a simple picture or shape on their paper, keeping it hidden from the other person. They then give only verbal instructions to the other person so that they can draw it, but without naming the shape or saying what the picture is. When they think they have finished, they compare drawings to see how successful their communication has been and what similarities, if any, there are between the two pictures.

Change roles and repeat the exercise.

Visual

Children's ability to see can be impaired in many different ways. These exercises give participants a chance to reflect on the use of a sense that many take for granted.

In pairs, blindfold one person. The partner then leads the blindfolded person around, inside or outside the building, enabling the blindfolded person to encounter a variety of obstacles like steps, changes of floor covering or different surfaces, in open spaces and in cluttered areas. The person guiding should lead the blindfolded person first with and then without spoken instructions to show how it feels to be completely dependent upon another.

Give each person in the group a pair of protective goggles or glasses smeared with Vaseline to give blurred and restricted vision. Then give them an activity to do, such as completing a jigsaw, making a simple meal (such as a jam sandwich), or doing a craft activity (such as colouring in and cutting out).

Auditory

Many children experience some level of hearing loss. For some children, the loss may be temporary; for others, it may be permanent. Conditions such as otitis media with effusion (OME), commonly known as glue ear, and ear infections mean that a child's ability to hear can vary. Children may have partial or complete deafness for many other reasons. The following exercises give participants a chance to reflect on the fact that many people take the sense of hearing for granted.

Split the group into two teams and ask each team to sit in a circle. Give one person in each team a prepared card with a sentence written on it (any sentence can be used, the more complex the better). Ask the person holding the card to whisper the sentence once to the person on their right. Repeat as fast as possible around the circle until the sentence is whispered back to the first person. How does the sentence compare to what was written on the card? How did you feel about the confusion, uncertainty, pressure and so on?

Next, split the group into pairs. Ask one person in each pair to place some earplugs in their ears; alternatively, use some headphones playing music. Ask each pair to try to hold a conversation.

Physical

There is a great variety of physical impairments, both temporary and permanent, which participants may have experienced themselves or within their groups. Many conditions produce unsteady gait or a tendency to be ponderous. Clumsiness is also a physical effect of conditions such as Down's Syndrome or cerebral palsy, and can result in some difficulty in grip and low manual dexterity.

The following exercises give just a brief insight into some of the concerns and issues that may affect children.

Borrow a wheelchair and take it in turns to push one another around in it. Include different surfaces, going up and down slopes and curbs, and being tilted. Think about how it would be to tackle these activities in church and in different groups, and how people may respond to someone in a wheelchair.

With bandages or tape, create a physical impairment, using the following suggestions:

❖ Strap the thumbs to the palms of the hand before trying to complete a task or activity, like preparing a simple meal or doing a craft. Place tape or strips of plaster so that there is still some movement of the fingers.
❖ Strap an arm to the body with a bandage (think about which arm to choose). Then ask participants to complete a task, a craft activity or some drawing.
❖ Strap a bandage around the legs and knees or arms and elbows, quite firmly, to restrict movement. With restricted leg movement, encounter a variety of obstacles such as steps, changes of floor covering or different surfaces, open spaces and cluttered areas. With restricted arm movement, try doing a craft activity or eating and drinking.

Dependency

Most participants will not, since childhood, have encountered a situation in which they need help to perform personal physical activities. This is something quite sensitive and any activities chosen for the group should be optional and presented sympathetically.

Give each person a pair of thick winter or gardening gloves to wear. Oversized ones are best, so that they don't fit properly. Offer a task or activity, such as a jigsaw, a craft, food to eat or clothes to put on.

In pairs, take it in turns to feed one another a simple meal and drink. Cereal and juice might be best. The person being fed is not to talk or help in any way.

Take a variety of items of clothing and, in pairs, take it in turns to dress one another. The person being dressed is not to talk or help in any way unless asked to do so.

Attitudes

Adults and children with special needs often find that they are treated differently or that people make assumptions about what help they need or the sort of person they are. Stereotyping and labelling are real dangers. Preconceptions and assumptions may need to be challenged. Children's workers need to be careful about how and why they treat people or communicate with them in the way they do.

To prepare for the exercise below, write some statements on Post-it notes. The statements are to highlight preconceptions and how they can alter our behaviour and affect the way people feel. Use statements such as the following:

❖ I cannot hear well
❖ I like to be hugged
❖ Speak slowly to me
❖ I don't like eye contact
❖ I am young
❖ I am old
❖ I am new
❖ Keep your distance
❖ Speak clearly
❖ I am nervous

Stand everyone in a line and place one of the Post-it notes on each person's forehead without letting them see what it says. The sticker will instruct the rest of the group how that person is to be treated during the exercise. The aim is for each person to guess what statement they have been given and to notice how they feel about the way they are treated.

Reflecting on current practice and working environment

Use a case study of a real situation, such as the one given below, to think about changes that can be made to improve both the environment and the situation.

Look at the case study individually or in small groups.

Case study

Three-year-old twin girls, Lauren and Megan, attend a preschool group every morning for two and a half hours. They both have very little speech and their behaviour is becoming more and more difficult for the staff and other children who attend. There are 15 children using one room with an outdoor play area.

As the girls arrive, there is a selection of activities for them to choose from: a roleplay and dressing-up corner, a garage, and several tables with a variety of activities set out, such as jigsaws, bead-threading and so on.

Lauren and Megan wander around, not really engaging with anything except the dressing-up clothes, which they dress in and continue to wander. As they wander, they occasionally pick things up and carry them around. Music is playing in the background while the children play.

An argument starts when Billie tries to take a phone from Megan. The argument becomes physical and Billie gets hurt. Staff members intervene and attempt to resolve things. They take the phone from Megan, give it to Billie and reprimand Megan.

A craft table is set up and the door is opened to the outdoor play area. The children are able to choose what they do. Megan and Lauren go outside to play. They play by themselves, making up their own games, sometimes copying the other children, and seem happier. This is the only time they play with other children.

The children all come in for snack time. Tables are prepared with juice and a snack for each child. Megan and Lauren sit for a short time but soon begin strolling around the room. As they wander, they sometimes reach into other children's bowls, taking their food. This causes some upset and further fighting. The girls are reprimanded once more.

Once everything is cleared away, the chairs are moved into a circle for a story and singing. The girls only partially engage with the story but really enjoy the singing. However, they tend to wander throughout both activities.

✤ What changes would you make to improve the situation?
✤ Does the case study remind you of anything about your group?
✤ Background music and too much choice were negative elements for Lauren and Megan. Is this true for some children in your group? What other things can be negative in your group, in your church or in other things you do?
✤ What other effects might arise from Lauren and Megan's lack of speech?
✤ In the argument over the phone, although Billie was in the wrong initially in trying to take a toy from someone else, it was only Megan who was reprimanded. Did you notice that? Why does that sort of thing happen?
✤ Are there any possible improvements for your group or church in the light of this case study?

Suggestions and changes

The case study above is taken from the notes made by an adviser invited to visit the children's group. Below are details of the actual alterations suggested by the adviser as a way to improve things.

✤ Introduce some form of communication aid, such as the Makaton vocabulary development project (MVDP). (See www.makaton.org for further information.) Such an aid should help to alleviate frustrations by helping the girls to communicate with others and enabling the staff to communicate more clearly with the girls.
✤ Create a pictorial timetable or pictures to help communicate the session structure, so that the girls can see clearly what is about to happen.
✤ Create a quiet corner with books and beanbags.
✤ Identify a member of staff at the beginning of each session who has a specific responsibility to support and supervise Megan and Lauren.
✤ Ensure that somebody greets the girls as they arrive and helps them engage with just one activity; otherwise there is too much choice and a lack of focus.
✤ The member of staff supporting the girls should try to observe constantly to see what precedes any behaviour that is a cause for concern. Often, it is in response to another child's action or behaviour and may be due to lack of communication or frustration. All staff should pause before intervening, to assess what is happening and not just to respond to the girls' behaviour.
✤ Play music only at specific times, not as background noise. It raises stress levels for some children.
✤ Staff need to agree and always use a consistent approach with the girls and follow things through.

The staff saw dramatic changes in the girls' behaviour quite quickly once the changes were made. They became more aware of the difficulties and frustrations and the reasons for the conflicts they were having. The development of a quiet corner proved very important. Megan and Lauren spent quite a lot of time looking at books together and their interpersonal skills improved (sharing, turn-taking and so on). They also began positive interactions with other children, although there were still occasional conflicts. More time outside was introduced when possible. This enabled the children to have more play space.

Because an identified member of staff was aware of the girls, that person was able to intervene before the conflicts became physical. He or she could see the full picture and could support the girls to respond to the situation appropriately. The identified member of staff was also able to be consistent and encourage the girls to sit and engage with an activity where appropriate. For Lauren and Megan, it did not need to be the same member of staff each day, thus avoiding any dependency issues. However, some children need more consistency and need to be able to form a relationship with the same member of staff.

✤ What strikes you as new or significant?
✤ What qualities are highlighted here as important for children's workers?

Learning styles and environments

Understanding how people learn and take in information enables us to make activities more inclusive by providing something for each of the learning styles. There is information about learning styles in the 'Programme planning' module of *Core Skills for Children's Work* (page 48).

As well as individual learning styles, the environment and external stimuli may have an effect upon each person—how they learn, react and respond—as well as the group and its dynamics.

Individually, think about a place of work, college, shop, library or church.

✤ What do you dislike about it?
✤ What would you change if you could?
✤ What difference would this change make and how would it benefit you or the people using the environment?

Support

Support for the child and his or her family is very important. It needs to be child-centred and individual, which can bring difficulties if not handled with sensitivity. This exercise is designed to help you to identify some of the many ways in which a person can be supported.

It is also important to be aware of what resources may be available to enable a child to participate fully as part of the group. Further information and support for the workers may also be helpful, and knowing where to find them is essential. Once again, this exercise should help you to identify where to find further information and support.

As a whole group, think about how best to support a child. List the different ways in which support can be given. For example, does the child need…

✤ supervision?
✤ physical assistance or adaptations?
✤ reassurance, or just somebody to be aware of them?

Also, think about how you can find out what sort of help a child needs. Remember always to ask first if a child seems to need help; sometimes it may just be time that is needed.

Divide into small groups. Ask each group to make a list on flip chart paper of the different material and resources that could be used or are available, not forgetting people within the group and those known by the group—perhaps people from the congregation who have similar needs or face some of the same difficulties regularly. Include suggestions of how and where to find further information such as learning aids, posters, books and websites, as well as practical resources such as information on where to purchase aids and adaptations that might enable somebody to participate fully in a session.

In turn, invite each group to present a list. Conclude with a general discussion and sharing of ideas.

Conflict

Being able to manage difficult situations or resolve conflict, whether it is between children, workers or with families, is an important aspect of working with people. You need to decide how you would work together if there were differing views on what was best for a child. How would you handle conflict between children?

As a whole group, list some of the sorts of disagreements or conflicts that might arise. Then divide into small groups of three or four. Each group takes one of the areas of conflict and discusses different ways in which it could be resolved. The suggestions are then presented to the whole group, either in a drama or as a dialogue. Further discussions could consider alternative outcomes or how things could be managed differently.

Information

As everyone is different, knowing the child, his or her needs and how best to help or support him or her is essential. But what information is needed, how do you collect it, and where from?

Have some examples of consent forms or information profiles for people to look at. (See www.barnabasinchurches.org.uk/nsns for examples of registration and parental consent forms, and a signing in and out form.) Then, in small groups, think about what information you might need to know about the child, his or her family and needs, and how best to offer support. Finally, devise an example of a consent form and a form to be used for gathering and storing information.

Complete an audit of your group

The following questions may be answered during the session. Alternatively, people could take the questions away to complete at a later date. The questions are designed to help workers to think more about their children's group, the people who are part of it, and the environment.

✦ Describe the physical, learning and social environment of your group. How accessible and welcoming is each environment?
✦ Are the first few moments in the group a positive or negative experience? Is it the same for everyone?
✦ What choices do children make? How are the choices offered?
✦ What sound or level of noise is in the background?
✦ What changes of pace or style take place in the group's time together?
✦ How do you know how the children feel?
✦ How is help offered or made available to children?
✦ Is there enough adult help?
✦ Do some children get too little or too much help?
✦ How do children meet each other's needs?
✦ How are children and young people involved in planning?
✦ How do you assess the needs of the children and young people?
✦ What registration process do you have?
✦ Do you have any consent forms?
✦ What do you consider to be best practice?

See www.brf.org.uk/pdf/special_needs.pdf for a downloadable leaflet designed to give leaders some useful tips on how best to support a child in their group with special needs.

Biblical thought

The great banquet

Read Luke 14:15–24. Use your imagination. What would a really great party be like? Reflect on the sights, sounds, smells, feelings and tastes. What is so unexpected about this story and why were the religious authorities so critical?

There are other passages in Luke's Gospel where Jesus is criticised for eating with people on the outside of society, such as Levi and his friends (5:27–31), and Zacchaeus (19:1–10). Who do the people who are 'poor or crippled or blind or lame' in the parable of the great banquet represent? (14:21). How do you understand such people as being made in God's image (Genesis 1:26)?

As Christians, we believe that everyone is invited to worship and play, sing and dance, and reflect on and celebrate the word of God. How does the picture Jesus paints in the parable of the great banquet help us to reflect on the requirement to be all-embracing and all-inclusive, especially to children with special needs?

What does this story tell us about God's love and the way God treats each person? How would we see God making his guests feel special at this banquet?

There is an emerging disability theology, which focuses the Church's thinking on 'the glory of the broken body of the risen Christ'—the risen Christ in heaven has a body with impairments. (See, for example, *The Disabled God: Toward a Liberatory Theology of Disability* by Nancy Eisland, Abingdon Press, 1995.)

The Body of Christ (meaning the Church rather than Jesus of Nazareth) is one where every part is important and we should take special care of those parts that seem to be the least important (1 Corinthians 12:12–27). In other words, if we put the marginalised (and clearly this applies to disabled people in our society) at the centre of our theology, then we are all changed and we can all know God better. This does not mean, of course, that we see disabled people only in terms of the less important or weaker parts of the Body of Christ: there is more to the image than that!

This exciting and challenging theology goes further than simply exploring the stories in which Jesus treated disabled people with respect. Many disabled people would say that the Church has much to learn. The Equalities and Diversity Project Officer of the Methodist Church recently said, 'Every disabled person who has spoken to me about their exclusion/inclusion in church has been told at some time or another that their impairment is a result of sin, or that if they had more faith they could be healed. Every single person!' We must take care that disabled children do not hear that message in our groups.

Reflection on learning

One of the learning outcomes of this module is an overview of special needs. What strikes you as particularly relevant to your work? Is there anything that you feel you want to learn more about?

Worship

Flowers

Have available a bunch of flowers, including a variety of different types of flowers. Give each person within the group a single flower from the bunch. As people look at the flower they have been given, ask them to study it in detail. Is the stem smooth or rough? Is it straight or curved? Are there any leaves and, if so, what is the shape? Look at the petals. What shape are they? Are the petals the same colour throughout and, if not, in what way does the colour change? How does the flower feel? How does it smell? As you look at it, can you see any blemishes or imperfections, or parts that are missing or broken?

Consider the care with which the flower you are holding was designed and made, the colours, textures, smells and its individuality.

In the same way that flowers are all different, so are we. There are often imperfections in us; sometimes parts of us are missing, broken or blemished.

The Bible tells us that our worth is above everything else in creation (Matthew 6:26–29). God created us and cares for us; we are made in his image and each one of us is special and individually made.

Light a candle and place it in the middle of the group. Invite everyone to lay the piece of paper with his or her 'I am special' descriptions (or his or her flower from the bunch) on the floor around the candle. Invite the group to spend some time in quiet reflection, thinking about the qualities that make each person special and individual. Bring to mind the children with whom the group members work, and think about the qualities that make each one of them special and individual. Close with the following prayer.

God of all life, who creates us and sustains us with love, thank you for creating each one of us to be special. Thank you for the individual qualities you have given us. Help us to see positive qualities in ourselves and in each other. Help us to see others through your eyes, and especially to care for the children we are thinking about today. Amen

Dyspraxia can affect movement and coordination, because brain messages are not properly transmitted to the body and messages from the senses are not properly relayed back to the brain. People who have dyspraxia often have difficulty coping with everyday tasks and may also have problems with language, perception and thought. The condition is fairly common in children and adults and used to be known as Clumsy Child Syndrome. It usually affects boys more than girls and up to one in 20 children suffer from dyspraxia. Having dyspraxia doesn't change a person's intelligence but it does affect how they learn and their ability to learn.

Dyspraxia affects a person's gross motor (large movement) and fine motor (small movement) skills and coordination. There may be a delay in reaching the normal milestones like sitting, standing, crawling, walking and talking, as physical movements and skills are often difficult to learn and maintain. Encouragement, repetition and support are needed for the person to learn new skills.

Poor balance means that there is a tendency to fall, trip or bump into things. There may be difficulty in riding bikes or participating in some sporting activities, such as running or ball games. Catching or hitting balls can be difficult because of poor hand-to-eye coordination and poor integration of the two sides of the body. People with dyspraxia may have flat feet or poor posture, clumsy gait and weak muscle tone, so they may have floppy or unstable joints and experience difficulty in standing for long periods or running, going up or down stairs or dancing. Children with dyspraxia often avoid joining in with sport or games because of their lack of coordination.

People often experience a lack of manual dexterity and difficulty in gripping things, thus finding activities like writing, drawing and craft difficult. It may also be difficult to carry out tasks that require both hands, such as tying shoelaces, fastening clothes or using cutlery. Some people are oversensitive to light or noise and find it difficult to distinguish sounds from background noise. Speech may be unclear and some people with dyspraxia may have difficulty in pronouncing some words. People with dyspraxia may also have difficulty concentrating on one thing for more than a few minutes or following more than one instruction at a time, as they have a poor attention span.

Children with dyspraxia tend to do much better on a one-to-one basis. They are often immature in their behaviour and understanding, and are inclined to take things literally. People with dyspraxia may have difficulty in planning and organising thoughts and understanding logic and reason. Poor memory means that they may forget or lose things. Many of the problems people with dyspraxia experience may lead to feelings of anxiety, frustration, low self-esteem and emotional outbursts.

Many of these characteristics are not unique to people with dyspraxia. Also, someone with dyspraxia may experience significant coordination and perceptual difficulties, but they will not experience all of the characteristics noted above. Everyone is different.

Useful websites

For more information, visit:

www.nhsdirect.nhs.uk
www.cafamily.org.uk
www.dyspraxiafoundation.org.uk
www.bbc.co.uk/health/conditions (search under 'D' for dyspraxia)

Reproduced with permission from *More Core Skills for Children's Work* published by BRF 2010 (978 1 84101 700 6) www.barnabasinchurches.org.uk

Down's Syndrome handout

Down's Syndrome is a genetic condition—that is, something a person is born with. It is the most common chromosomal disorder.

Human cells normally contain 23 pairs of chromosomes, the parts of body cells that carry inherited information. In each pair, there is one chromosome from the mother and one from the father. People with Down's Syndrome have an extra chromosome 21. This can mean that a child's development is likely to be delayed or impaired, both physically and mentally, resulting in learning difficulties and health problems. Some are more severely affected than others. They may develop in stops and starts. Often, a child with Down's Syndrome will not start to use language until his or her third year and may use some sign language before talking.

People with Down's Syndrome have many different characteristics. Although each person is different and individuals will not experience all of the characteristics, some of the following physical features may be present. With treatment and support, the average life expectancy of someone with Down's Syndrome is about 60 years.

✤ Babies with Down's Syndrome usually have a lower than average birth weight and gain weight slower. They are usually shorter than average as adults.

✤ Babies and children with Down's Syndrome may have poor muscle tone (hypotonia) and loose joints. This muscular floppiness occurs in the limbs and neck and usually improves with age.

✤ People with Down's Syndrome often have a rounded face and a small nose with a flatter bridge. The back of the head is slightly flattened (this is called brachycephaly) and some people have smaller than average ears, increasing the risk of infections.

✤ Babies and young children with Down's Syndrome tend to be prone to chest and sinus infections.

✤ In people with Down's Syndrome, the eyes tend to slant upwards and often have an extra fold of skin, which can increase the risk of eye infections.

✤ Children with Down's Syndrome often have straight, soft hair. As children, they may have an extra fold of skin over the back of the neck and, as adults, short, broad necks.

✤ People with Down's Syndrome often have a smaller than average mouth, giving the appearance of a larger or protruding tongue, sometimes causing difficulties in eating or drinking.

✤ The hands may be broad, with a single crease across the palm, and short fingers. The feet are often stubby, with a wide space between the first and second toes.

✤ Dry skin can be a problem, needing regular moisturising to prevent cracking and infections.

✤ About one in three children born with Down's Syndrome has a heart defect. The severity varies: some defects are quite minor, such as heart murmurs, while some are severe, requiring medication and/or surgery. People working with Down's children need to know whether the particular child has a heart problem because overexertion can have dramatic effects. They need to know what to do to prevent a potentially serious condition from occurring.

✤ A number of medical problems are more common in those with Down's Syndrome. Many have stomach or intestinal complaints, which can make eating difficult, and thyroid gland problems. Other physical problems include cataracts, hearing and sight difficulties and a susceptibility to infection.

✤ People with Down's Syndrome have varying degrees of learning disability, which may range from moderate to severe.

Useful websites

For more information, visit:

www.nhsdirect.nhs.uk
www.cafamily.org.uk
www.downs-syndrome.org.uk

Reproduced with permission from *More Core Skills for Children's Work* published by BRF 2010 (978 1 84101 700 6) www.barnabasinchurches.org.uk

Autistic spectrum disorder handout

Autistic spectrum disorder (ASD) is the name of a group of disorders, including autism and Asperger syndrome. 'Spectrum' describes the range of characteristics of the condition, which vary widely from mild to severe.

People who have Asperger syndrome tend to be more able and have average or above average intelligence, but still have difficulty making sense of the world and experience communication difficulties. People with autism are usually more severely disabled and may also have a learning disability. Conversely, people with autism are sometimes found to have an exceptional skill, such as an aptitude for drawing, mathematics or playing a musical instrument. Boys are more likely to be affected than girls. Autistic spectrum disorder is a lifelong developmental condition.

People with ASD have a different perspective on and experience of the world. The characteristics of the disorder vary from person to person, but ASD affects how a person communicates with and relates to other people. The traits of ASD can be divided into the following three main groups.

Difficulties with social interaction

People with autism tend to be socially isolated and have difficulty forming social relationships. They may seem distant or uncaring to others. They are unaware of what is socially appropriate and find it very difficult to develop friendships and relate to others.

Problems with verbal and non-verbal communication

People with autism have difficulty understanding feelings, emotions and vague concepts. They are unable to give what is considered appropriate eye contact and have difficulty in understanding gestures, body language, facial expressions and tone of voice, making it difficult for them to empathise with other people's feelings.

Social imagination impairments

People with autism have difficulty in the development of play and imagination, and find it hard to take part in 'pretend' play. They prefer routine and dislike changes, often repeating a game rigidly.

Some of the typical difficulties of autistic spectrum disorders are as follows:

* Repetitive behaviour, such as hand flapping or spinning and resistance to changes in routine
* Obsessions with particular objects, games or routines
* Poor coordination
* Difficulties with fine movement control (especially in Asperger syndrome)
* Absence of normal facial expression and body language
* Lack of eye contact
* Tendency to spend time alone, finding it difficult to make friends
* Lack of imaginative play
* Difficulty using verbal and non-verbal skills
* Difficulty understanding instructions
* Varying concentration levels
* Oversensitivity to specific things like touch, certain textures, light levels or sound

It is important to remember that everyone is an individual and will have very different characteristics and needs. Characteristics may also change at different stages of a person's life.

Useful websites

For more information, visit:

www.nhsdirect.nhs.uk
www.cafamily.org.uk
www.nas.org.uk
www.bbc.co.uk/health/conditions (search under 'A' for autism)

Visual impairment handout

The term 'visual impairment' is used to describe anyone who is blind or partially sighted, with a degree of loss or distortion of vision. People who are sight impaired or partially sighted have a serious loss of sight, but are not blind. A person can register as sight impaired or partially sighted if they can read only the top letter of an optician's chart from six metres or less, even when wearing glasses or lenses.

Some people will be affected by a sight problem from birth, while others may inherit an eye condition. Some people may lose their sight as the result of an accident, while illness can lead to conditions. Sight loss can be sudden and severe, but it is more common for deterioration to occur over a long period of time, with distant objects slowly becoming more difficult to recognise or distinguish.

People are affected by eye conditions in different ways. Being blind or partially sighted does not always mean that a person is living in total darkness. Some people have a perception of light; others can recognise a friend or an object at arm's length. Also, the degree of vision varies from person to person. Some people will have no central vision or no vision to the sides; others may see a patchwork of blank and defined areas, or everything may be seen as a vague blur.

With some eye conditions, as well as a reduction in vision other symptons may be present, such as eye pain, a burning or gritty sensation, fogginess or distortion.

Useful websites

For more information, visit:

www.nhsdirect.nhs.uk
www.cafamily.org.uk
www.rnib.org.uk
www.actionforblindpeople.org.uk

Reproduced with permission from *More Core Skills for Children's Work* published by BRF 2010 (978 1 84101 700 6) www.barnabasinchurches.org.uk

Hearing impairment handout

Hearing impairment, or deafness, is when a person's hearing is affected by a disease, disorder or injury. There are a number of different reasons why someone might be deaf or lose their hearing. Age, noise, genetics, illness, head injury or other ear problems such as wax, damaged eardrum or inflammation are some of the causes of hearing impairment.

The hearing loss can be permanent or temporary. Hearing loss can be present at birth or develop in childhood or adulthood. Some people experience a sudden, profound loss of hearing, perhaps because of a viral infection or an injury to their head or ears. Others experience a gradual decrease in their hearing over a long period of time. Some causes of hearing impairment have symptoms other than hearing loss, such as dizziness, whistling sounds in the ears and loss of balance or coordination.

Hearing is important for the development of speech and language. There are two different types of hearing loss. The first is when something interferes with the transmission of sound from the outer ear to the inner ear (conductive hearing loss). The second is when there is a problem with the messages (pathway) from the inner ear to the brain, or something wrong with the inner ear (sensorineural hearing loss).

There are different levels of hearing impairment, which can vary widely from person to person. Some people have partial hearing loss, which means that the ear can pick up some sounds; others have moderate hearing loss, severe hearing loss or complete hearing loss, which means that the ear cannot hear at all. In some types of hearing loss, a person can experience much more difficulty when there is background noise. One or both ears may be affected and the impairment may be worse in one ear than in the other.

Treatment for hearing loss varies depending upon the cause of the hearing impairment. It might involve removing wax or dirt from the ear canal or treating an underlying infection. It may require surgery if there is damage, or to place grommets or to insert a hearing aid or cochlear implant.

There are different types of hearing aids, some of which are fitted externally and some internally. Hearing aids are designed to enable people to hear more clearly and can be adjusted to individuals' needs. People with severe hearing loss will usually need to rely on lip-reading or sign language, even with a hearing aid.

Useful websites

For more information, visit:

www.nhsdirect.nhs.uk
www.cafamily.org.uk
www.rnid.org.uk
www.ndcs.org.uk
www.bda.org.uk

Cerebral palsy handout

Cerebral palsy is a description of a physical impairment that affects movement, posture and coordination. It is a condition, not a disease or an illness, and is caused by damage to the cerebrum before, during or after birth. The cerebrum is the largest part of the brain and is involved with the senses (such as sight and hearing), voluntary movements of the muscles, thinking and communication. Cerebral palsy affects different people in different ways. Some people's movements may be affected slightly, while others are affected very severely.

There are three main types of cerebral palsy.

✤ **Spastic cerebral palsy**: People with spastic cerebral palsy have some muscle stiffness and weakness, which affects their range and control of movements and the flexibility of their joints.
✤ **Athetoid cerebral palsy**: People with athetoid (or dyskinetic) cerebral palsy have some loss of control of their posture or movements: their muscles stiffen involuntarily and they make unwanted movements. Athetoid cerebral palsy often affects speech and hearing.
✤ **Ataxic cerebral palsy**: People with ataxic cerebral palsy have problems with balance and coordination.

The main effect of cerebral palsy is difficulty in movement, the inability to control movement properly, and moving or jerking uncontrollably. Many people with cerebral palsy are hardly affected; others have problems with walking, feeding, talking or using their hands. Tightness of the muscles may affect the limbs: they start to become fixed in abnormal positions because some muscle groups are stronger than others. The ankles tend to be straightened out, as if trying to walk on tiptoe, and arms are bent at the elbow and wrist. The paralysis or palsy may affect mainly the legs or all four limbs or just one side of the body. People with cerebral palsy almost always have difficulty in walking, which varies from very slight to total.

Sometimes other parts of the brain may also be affected, causing problems with:

✤ speech (due to lack of control of the muscles in the throat or mouth)
✤ epilepsy (one in three children with cerebral palsy has fits or seizures)
✤ balance and coordination
✤ hearing and sight
✤ controlling movements, sitting upright or maintaining other positions
✤ perception
✤ learning

Some people have severe muscular problems while others have slight learning difficulties. Most people are somewhere in the middle. However, it is important to note that not all people with cerebral palsy have learning difficulties.

There is no cure for cerebral palsy but there are plenty of treatments and therapies that can reduce the impact of the condition. Physiotherapy, occupational therapy and speech therapy can all play an important part, as well as medication or surgery to ease symptoms such as muscle spasticity. Therapies help with posture and movement, to prevent progression of disability and to overcome everyday difficulties.

With help, most people with cerebral palsy are able to live much the same sort of life as everyone else in terms of school, friends, hobbies and sports, building a career and having a family. They may have to work a bit harder to overcome practical problems, but most things are possible.

Useful websites

For more information, visit:

www.nhsdirect.nhs.uk
www.cafamily.org.uk
www.scope.org.uk/information/cp.shtml
www.bbc.co.uk/health/conditions (search under 'C' for cerebral palsy)

Reproduced with permission from *More Core Skills for Children's Work* published by BRF 2010 (978 1 84101 700 6) www.barnabasinchurches.org.uk

Personal reflection sheet

What did you learn from this session?

How will this affect the way you work with children?

What further items in this area would you like to follow up?

Portfolio checklist

Learning outcomes

❖ To gain an overview of some of the different needs people may have.

❖ To develop an awareness of issues and difficulties faced by children with disabilities.

❖ To reflect on current practice and working environments.

❖ To explore ways to enable a child to participate fully in activities.

To show that the learning outcomes have been achieved, your portfolio must include at least the following. *(Tick when you have included each one in the file.)*

☐ Personal reflection sheet

☐ Notes taken during the module, with any additional ideas

☐ Your list of what is special about you

☐ Your ideas about what is helpful or unhelpful in relation to particular special needs

☐ Answers from yourself and your group in response to the case study

☐ The audit of your own children's group

☐ Your thoughts on the biblical passage used, or another of your own choice

☐ Your flower

☐ Any other answers and/or reflections you wish to include

The participant's involvement in a group for More CORE Session 2, 'Special Needs', is confirmed. The learning outcomes have been achieved through the evidence provided.

Signed (assessor) _____ Date _____

Any comments from assessor

Signed (candidate) _____ Date _____

MORE CORE SESSION THREE
Challenging behaviour

Aim

To explore issues around challenging behaviour and to identify mechanisms for dealing with challenging behaviour.

Learning outcomes

❖ To clarify what is meant by disruptive or 'bad' behaviour.
❖ To know how to look for the cause(s) behind the behaviour.
❖ To become more aware of the attitudes and behaviours of adults.
❖ To explore different strategies for dealing with behavioural issues.

Materials needed

Starters

✳ Agitators: a 12- to 16-piece child's jigsaw
✳ 'Perceptions' PowerPoint presentation
   (download from www.coreskillsforchurches.com/2367)

CORE

✳ Essential/Desirable/Unacceptable chart (see page 56)
✳ Enough blank cards for each group member to have three or four cards each; pens or pencils; Blu-Tack, masking tape, or a basket
✳ 'Challenging behaviour' scenarios (see page 57)
✳ 'Understanding the behaviour' shopkeeper's account (see page 58) and mother's perspective (see page 59)
✳ Lining wallpaper or similar; pens or pencils
✳ Relationships: 15 tips (see page 60)

Biblical thought

✳ An image of the painting *Christ discovered in the temple* by Simone Martini, 1342
   (see www.liverpoolmuseums.org.uk/walker/collections/13c-16c/discovered.asp)

Worship

✳ A selection of Bibles in different versions

Opening thought

Save me, Lord God! Hurry and help.
Psalm 70:1

We should listen to the behaviour because sometimes the behaviour is the only language children have.
Alice Miller

Starters

Agitator

> **You will need:**
> * A 12- to 16-piece child's jigsaw

Either:

Prime one member of the group to be an 'agitator'. This person should refuse to cooperate with the group in one of the following ways.

* Turn their chair round to face away from the group, and refuse to speak.
* Persistently whistle or talk while others are talking.
* Tap a pen or book noisily on the table or chair leg.

Or:

Provide the group with a simple 12- to 16-piece child's jigsaw, giving each person a selection of pieces. The objective is to work together to build the picture, following two simple rules.

* No one must speak or try to communicate with sign language or gestures throughout the exercise.
* Group members may only touch the pieces they have been given (although they may choose to give a piece to another member to place).

Arrange in advance for a co-leader or other group member to be an agitator and break one of these rules throughout the exercise, either by talking or taking other pieces, or just refusing to place their pieces.

Debrief

Whichever exercise you choose, it is important to debrief, to allow the agitator to come back into the group and to ensure that the group can work together without resentment.

* How did one person's refusal to join in affect the group?
* How did the group respond to the non-cooperative member?
* Was the behaviour 'bad'?
* How did the agitator feel?
* How did the group feel?

Expectations

Make a quick list under each of the four headings below. Discuss your list in groups of three or four. Consider the whole purpose of your children's group, not just behaviour.

* What do we expect of children in our group?
* What do children expect of leaders in our group?
* What does the rest of the church expect of our group?
* What does God expect of our group?

What are the key differences between your four sets of answers? Have you ever asked the children in your group such questions?

Perceptions

> **You will need:**
> * 'Perceptions' PowerPoint presentation

Look at the images on the PowerPoint. Write down what you see. Do the exercise in silence with a few seconds for each slide. At the end, share your answers and find out if you all saw the same thing.

Learning points

We don't always see the same thing as other people—and, like an iceberg, there may be much more under the surface than is visible to the eye. When children display challenging behaviour, there is always a reason for that behaviour. You can only deal with the behaviour once you have dealt with the cause.

If the group does not keep silent through this exercise, point out that we sometimes don't adhere completely to instructions given. How can we expect children to adhere completely to all our instructions all the time if we can't keep simple instructions ourselves?

CORE

Bad behaviour _____

What do we mean by 'bad' behaviour? Ask the group individually to draw up lists of actions that would be classed as 'bad' behaviour in your children's group, then mark the five worst and five least worst.

In groups of three or four:

❖ Share your lists.
❖ Discuss what would be most likely to cause the five 'least worst' behaviours you have identified, and therefore who is responsible for the occurrence of these actions.

All together, discuss your findings and then the following suggestions.

❖ Behaviour that is acceptable in some groups is not acceptable in others.
❖ There is a reason behind bad behaviour: it is not simply that the children themselves are 'bad'.
❖ Some so-called 'bad' behaviour is the result of children not meeting standards set by adults, and such standards may not be appropriate in the first place.
❖ Actions that are dangerous must be minimised or prevented.

In the same groups of three or four, discuss the five worst behaviours on your list.

❖ Are any of them 'dangerous' behaviour?
❖ What steps can we take to minimise the risk of these actions taking place?
❖ What sanctions do we use or could we use in relation to them?

All together, discuss your findings and then the following key steps in minimising bad behaviour.

❖ Identify potentially dangerous behaviours.
❖ Identify the risks involved, such as those posed by the building, the people or the nature of the activity.
❖ When unacceptable actions occur, find out the reason for the action.
❖ Take steps to minimise the recurrence of the action.

Essential/Desirable/Unacceptable ___

You will need:
✳ An Essential/Desirable/Unacceptable chart for each group member (p. 56).

Give each group member a copy of the chart and invite them individually to fill it in. In pairs, discuss your answers.

Agreeing the boundaries _____

If you did the 'Expectations' exercise as a starter, use the results in the following discussion. If not, make a list now, answering the following questions.

❖ What do leaders expect of children in our group?
❖ What do children expect of leaders in our group?

Put your lists alongside one another. Is there any disparity? Should some items be on both lists? Do the leaders' expectations include 'having fun'? Do the leaders expect that children will want to be there? (They may not: parental pressure may have brought them along!)

Some of the differences between the lists may explain why you are encountering certain kinds of behaviour. For example, if adults expect children to sit still and the children expect fun and games, fidgeting is the very least outcome that can be expected!

It might be worth trying to do this exercise with the group of children that you work with. Together you could then work out a list of agreed expectations. (This method might be more positive than trying to make a list of agreed 'rules', which could deteriorate into a long list of 'Do Not's.)

Once you have decided on a list of expectations, it could be used as the basis for a community agreement that becomes owned by the whole group of adults and children. The agreement could be printed and displayed so that adults and children can refer to it. If it is to be a worthwhile tool for managing behaviour, it will need to be consulted often.

Another method would be to look at other group agreements and discuss which items you agree with and which you disagree with. Group members could add or delete items.

Every group of children's workers needs to meet together and decide what they agree to be essential, desirable and unacceptable behaviours. Unless this has been done, children will enjoy playing one adult against another.

Responding to challenging behaviour

> **You will need:**
> * Enough blank cards for each group member to have three or four cards each
> * Pens or pencils
> * Blu-Tack, masking tape or a basket

Give each group member three or four cards and invite them to write on each card an example of challenging behaviour that they have encountered. The cards should then be placed on a suitable wall or board or collected in a basket. Ask everyone to take three cards and, in groups of two or three, discuss what an appropriate response should be. For example:

❖ Deliberately breaking a window: exclusion.
❖ Kicking a partner's chair: quiet request from leader to stop.

When everyone is back together, discuss the cards still in the basket and report back on the small group's discussion. Then talk about how the consequences of particular behaviours can be communicated to a group of children. Make sure the following aspects are covered:

❖ Consistent practice by all involved.
❖ Colour card systems (giving examples if no one has experience of this).
❖ Consequences forming part of the community agreement.

Scenarios

> **You will need:**
> * 'Challenging behaviour' scenarios (p. 57) for each group member

Give each group member a copy of the list. Invite them to consider the scenarios and then list the words and actions they would use in response to each one.

There are many possible reasons for unacceptable behaviour. The list below may explain the behaviour in the scenarios, but the group may wish to add to it.

❖ Code of behaviour not agreed with children.
❖ Programme of activity not well enough organised.
❖ Level of activity not appropriate to child.

❖ Material not easily understood.
❖ Inappropriate room layout.
❖ Issues outside the group, such as problems at home, medical conditions and so on.

Understanding the behaviour

> **You will need:**
> * 'Understanding the behaviour' stories (pp. 58 and 59)

Read the introduction below, then split into small groups and give out copies of the shopkeeper's account. The participants should read it and discuss their responses. After about ten minutes, give out copies of the mother's account so that participants can again read and respond in the groups. Does the mother's perspective alter your views? If so, how?

Finally, discuss the whole exercise with everyone together.

Introduction

Challenging behaviour often seems to make little sense. A young person might wreck an activity that they have previously been participating in happily or fight with or hurt friends or people they care for.

If we impose a rational, adult explanation on these behaviours, we must conclude that the young people are either irrational or are driven by some deep-seated urge to frustrate and undermine the good intentions of anyone who tries to help them. In short, they seem to be either mad or very, very bad.

How does it work for the young person?

Someone who finds it difficult to concentrate on academic tasks might throw material, disrupt the group or walk away whenever presented with a structured task. The adolescent boy ignored at home or overshadowed by a sibling might act up in group situations or isolate himself.

Each behaviour must be understood in terms of the young person concerned and the situation in which it occurs. It is often suggested that behaviours occur because the young person is trying to control or manage the situation. This is extremely rare. It is much more likely that they have little or no idea about how to influence a given situation, so they are making a last-ditch attempt at avoiding, or changing in some way, a situation that they find confusing or disturbing. This is important for us to understand because it may mean that the sequence of events that, from an adult perspective, leads to a particular outcome (such as exclusion from the club) might be poorly understood by the young person.

We should listen to the behaviour, because sometimes behaviour is the only language children have.

Alice Miller

Relationships

> You will need:
> ✳ Lining wallpaper or similar
> ✳ Pens or pencils
> ✳ Relationships: 15 tips (p. 60)

Individually, or in a small group, draw an outline of a child. Decide what age the child is. Around the figure, write or draw what pressures the child might be under, such as school performance, peer acceptability, managing a two-household family, learning difficulties, physical needs and so on. Discuss the following questions in a group.

✤ How might particular circumstances or pressures show in behaviour?
✤ Why is it helpful to know this?
✤ Does it mean that we should ignore unacceptable behaviour? For example, if the child is being bullied and then in turn bullies others, what should we do?
✤ Does behaviour sometimes get in the way of relationships?

Learning to manage ourselves helps with difficult behaviour and builds relationships. Give out the 'Relationships: 15 tips' sheet. Give the group time to read through the list and then, in twos or threes, invite individuals to reflect on their own behaviour and their response to the behavioural tips.

Biblical thought

Jesus in the temple

> You will need:
> ✳ An image of the painting *Christ discovered in the temple* by Simone Martini, 1342 (see www.liverpoolmuseums.org.uk/walker/ collections/13c-16c/discovered.asp)

Read Luke 2:41–52, about Jesus in the temple. Jesus' behaviour in this story might certainly be defined as 'challenging'. If possible, examine the painting *Christ discovered in the temple* by Simone Martini (1342).

If you could add speech bubbles to each of the characters in the painting, what would they be saying? How might this story help our thinking about challenging behaviour?

Reflection on learning

Relationships are vital in children's work, and behaviour is crucial to relationships. Has this session made you think of anything you want to do to improve your relationships with the children or the other leaders?

What changes will you now consider making in your children's group in order to improve the children's behaviour or the smooth running of your sessions?

Worship

Read Ephesians 6:1–4 in two or three translations, including *THE MESSAGE* (see below).

Children, do what your parents tell you. This is only right. 'Honour your father and mother' is the first commandment that has a promise attached to it, namely, 'so you will live well and have a long life'. Fathers, don't exasperate your children by coming down hard on them. Take them by the hand and lead them in the way of the Master.

Share your thoughts on this passage. What lessons does it have for us? In *THE MESSAGE* Eugene Peterson interprets the passage as an instruction to fathers not to 'exasperate your children by coming down hard on them', but rather to 'take them by the hand and lead them in the way of the Master'.

How do we 'exasperate' children and what is the best way to 'lead them in the way of the Master'?

Think of the most difficult children you know. Write down three positive things about each child. Pray for them.

Useful resources

If you have children with special needs in your group, there is an excellent resource in Simon Bass' book *Special Children, Special Needs (Sure Foundations)* (Church House Publishing, 2003)

A story book that may give pause for thought about right or wrong behaviour is *Six Dinner Sid* by Inga Moore (Hodder Children's Books, 2004).

Essential/Desirable/Unacceptable chart

Fill in the following chart.

	ESSENTIAL	DESIRABLE	UNACCEPTABLE
Interrupting when the leader is speaking	❏	❏	❏
Writing neatly	❏	❏	❏
Swearing	❏	❏	❏
Attending every week	❏	❏	❏
Eating worksheets	❏	❏	❏
Hitting other children	❏	❏	❏
Always volunteering to give out equipment	❏	❏	❏

Reproduced with permission from *More Core Skills for Children's Work* published by BRF 2010 (978 1 84101 700 6) www.barnabasinchurches.org.uk

Challenging behaviour scenarios

1. You meet an angry parent who wants to 'see someone in charge'.
   How would you respond? Words? Actions?

2. You give a child a simple instruction. He or she refuses to do as you have asked,
   saying, 'No I'm not, and you can't make me.'
   How would you respond? Words? Actions?

3. Your group will not listen to you because they are more interested in what's going on
   in another group.
   How would you respond? Words? Actions?

4. You hear a group of children swearing.
   How would you respond? Words? Actions?

5. Children keep talking when you need them to listen.
   How would you respond? Words? Actions?

6. A child swears at you when you ask him or her to do something.
   How would you respond? Words? Actions?

7. One of the other helpers is in difficulty with one of the children.
   How would you respond? Words? Actions?

8. One of the children has got into trouble for something you know they did not do.
   How would you respond? Words? Actions?

9. You have a child in your group who is a bully.
   How would you respond? Words? Actions?

Reproduced with permission from *More Core Skills for Children's Work* published by BRF 2010 (978 1 84101 700 6) www.barnabasinchurches.org.uk

Shopkeeper's account

Some people just don't know how to bring up children. I still wonder if I should have reported the mother to Social Services.

They came in and looked so respectable. The child looked so sweet, angelic even, as if butter wouldn't melt in her mouth. But what came out of that mouth! She could only have been about seven or eight years old, but her language was dreadful. She could only have heard language like that at home. And her mother didn't even tell her off, just tried to get her to keep her voice down. Everyone was looking—well, I had quite a queue. And then, I couldn't believe it, the mother just took a fruit drink and gave it to her to drink there and then—trying to shut her up, I suppose. Then the little girl threw it all over the floor in a tantrum, so the mother gave her another bottle and helped herself to sweets. Then she just dropped some money on the counter and took the child out.

I think it's disgusting. People like that shouldn't be allowed to have children.

❖ What are your feelings, reading this account?
❖ What are your thoughts about:
  • the child?
  • the mother?
  • the shopkeeper?

If you were in the queue, how would you respond?

Reproduced with permission from *More Core Skills for Children's Work* published by BRF 2010 (978 1 84101 700 6) www.barnabasinchurches.org.uk

Understanding the behaviour: handout 2

Mother's perspective

It was so embarrassing, and I feel so guilty. It was a beautiful day and Abigail was having such a wonderful time on the beach, running about. I just didn't realise how late it was, not until Abigail started to show signs of being hyper. It was then I realised that I was late in giving her her insulin, and, to make things worse, when I opened the bag I realised that I had left the insulin in the caravan.

I just didn't know what I was going to do, but I remembered passing a sweet shop on the promenade, so I picked Abigail up and ran—I left all our things on the beach. When I got to the shop,

Abigail was in a real state, swearing and flailing about. The shop was packed. I couldn't get near the counter to explain to the shopkeeper, so I just got her a drink—only for her to have a major tick as soon as it was in her hand. So I got her another and a handful of sugary sweets, dropped three pound coins on the counter and fled.

I honestly can't imagine what people thought. Diabetes is bad enough on its own, but with Tourettes as well it can be a nightmare. I bet no one understood.

Reproduced with permission from *More Core Skills for Children's Work* published by BRF 2010 (978 1 84101 700 6) www.barnabasinchurches.org.uk

Relationships: 15 tips

1. Speak calmly and give clear and simple instructions.

2. Give children time to carry out instructions.

3. Keep your distance. Don't point, wag fingers or prod.

4. Be fair and consistent.

5. Use humour as appropriate.

6. Tell the children (and adults) how you want them to behave.

7. Separate the behaviour from the person. Never label children or call them 'bad'; refer to the behaviour instead.

8. Distract children before trouble begins if you can—start a conversation; walk alongside.

9. Notice good behaviour and comment or express appreciation.

10. Don't shout or use sarcasm or humiliation.

11. Report good behaviour to others.

12. Encourage responsibility, such as providing special roles or jobs.

13. Apologise when you make mistakes. It models respect and helps everyone.

14. Avoid confrontation with angry children, young people or adults. Stay calm and quiet and talk to them later when you and they are calm.

15. Know where to go for help and ask for it if you need it.

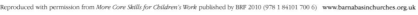

Reproduced with permission from *More Core Skills for Children's Work* published by BRF 2010 (978 1 84101 700 6) www.barnabasinchurches.org.uk

Personal reflection sheet

What did you learn from this session?

How will this affect the way you work with children?

What further items in this area would you like to follow up?

Reproduced with permission from *More Core Skills for Children's Work* published by BRF 2010 (978 1 84101 700 6) www.barnabasinchurches.org.uk

Portfolio checklist

Learning outcomes

❖ To clarify what is meant by disruptive or 'bad' behaviour.

❖ To learn how to look for the cause(s) behind the behaviour.

❖ To become more aware of the attitudes and behaviours of adults.

❖ To explore different strategies for dealing with behavioural issues.

To show that the learning outcomes have been achieved, your portfolio must include at least the following. *(Tick when you have included each one in the file.)*

☐ Personal reflection sheet

☐ Notes from discussions in this module

☐ Lists from the 'Expectations' starter exercise

☐ Completed 'Essential/Desirable/Unacceptable' behaviour chart

☐ A copy of your own code of behaviour for your group

☐ Your responses to the scenarios

☐ Any other responses or reflections you wish to include

The participant's involvement in a group for More Core Session 3, 'Challenging Behaviour', is confirmed. The learning outcomes have been evidenced through the portfolio provided.

Signed (assessor) _____ Date _____

Any comments from assessor

Signed (candidate) _____ Date _____

Reproduced with permission from *More Core Skills for Children's Work* published by BRF 2010 (978 1 84101 700 6) **www.barnabasinchurches.org.uk**

62 • MORE CORE SESSION 3: CHALLENGING BEHAVIOUR

The global dimension

Aim

To explore the ways that awareness of global issues and the international dimension to the Christian faith can enrich our work with children.

Learning outcomes

❖ To have an increased understanding of the ways in which the Christian faith is expressed and experienced around the world.
❖ To explore insights from other cultures and other perspectives on life and faith.
❖ To review the cultural content of current materials and practice and consider possible changes.
❖ To be more aware of the challenges and complexities of the global issues affecting children.
❖ To consider ways in which children can be involved in the Christian mission to care for and be engaged with God's world.
❖ To reflect on some Bible passages that relate to global issues.

Materials needed

Starters

✱ A ball of wool and a globe or map of the world
✱ Quiz: Global issues (see page 70)
✱ Information sheet: Global impact (see pages 71–72)
✱ Maps: Seeing the world differently (see pages 73–74)
✱ A selection of mission and aid magazines and some recent newspapers

CORE

✱ Cards: What can we do about poverty? (see page 75)
✱ 'Global dilemmas' discussion topics and background information (see pages 76–77)
✱ Case studies: Making connections (see pages 78–79)
✱ Cards: Bible stories relating to global issues (see page 80)
✱ 'Global voices' poems and quotations (see page 81)

Worship

✱ Song: 'He came down that we may have love' (*Sent by the Lord*, see www.ionabooks.com)
✱ Song: 'If you believe and I believe' (*Many and Great*, see www.ionabooks.com)
✱ Welcome liturgy from the Church of India (see page 82)
✱ *The Christ we share* pictures (see www.uspg.org.uk, www.cms-uk.org or www.mph.org.uk)
✱ *Jesus Mafa* paintings (see www.jesusmafa.com)
✱ Prayers and 'Sharing the peace' ideas from around the world (see pages 83–85)

Opening thought

After this, I saw a large crowd with more people than could be counted. They were from every race, tribe, nation and language. (Revelation 7:9)

Starters

A worldwide web

> You will need:
> ❋ A ball of wool
> ❋ A globe or large map of the world

Sit in a circle around a globe or map of the world. Invite each person to toss the ball of wool to another, holding on to her or his end in order to create a web of connections. Invite each person, as they do this, to name a country they have visited or where they have family or friends, or maybe a country that they know about and would like to visit.

More and more of us have travelled globally and have global connections. Global issues and links are taught and encouraged in primary schools. This is the world of children today.

You might like to demonstrate the 'butterfly's wings' effect with your web of wool. If one person tugs and then the person who feels that tug responds with a tug, soon the first person's tug will have been transmitted by everyone around the circle.

A world quiz

> You will need:
> ❋ Quiz: Global issues (p. 70)

Start by looking together at the definition of globalisation from Christian Aid below.

Globalisation is the term used to describe the increased pace of interconnectedness that has taken place over recent years. It came about as a result of two developments. Firstly, technological changes have enabled information and goods to travel much faster than before, making it easier to transport things and communicate with people. Secondly, the end of the cold war and the spread of a new political philosophy of liberalisation led to the removal of trade barriers. As a result of globalisation, foreign trade and investment have grown dramatically.

For more information on Christian Aid, please visit www.christianaid.org.uk

Globalisation is, however, an uneven and unequal process, affecting different countries in different ways. This results in huge inequalities in our world.

Give out copies of the 'Global issues' quiz. In groups, talk about the quiz and its impact upon yourself and the children you work with. How might the children you know respond to this quiz?

Global impact

> You will need:
> ❋ Information sheet: Global impact (pp. 71–72)

Globalisation affects many different aspects of life in our world. It has impacted us all, politically, socially, culturally, economically, technologically and environmentally.

Consider each of these areas in relation to children. How has globalisation affected their experience of and outlook on life?

Take another look

> You will need:
> ❋ Maps: Seeing the world differently, downloaded from the Internet (see pp. 73–74)

Study the different maps, with their varying perspectives and ways of representing countries according to land area, wealth, population and life expectancy. What different insights do these maps give us about how we view the world?

Global impressions

> You will need:
> ❋ A selection of mission and aid magazines
> ❋ Some recent newspapers

Distribute the magazines and newspapers to the group and then, in pairs, start looking for information about countries and churches outside the UK. Each pair should aim to report back on the following questions.

❖ Which countries were mentioned?
❖ What sort of picture is presented of each country? Is it presented well and is it fair?
❖ What, if anything, is said about the church in those countries?
❖ What is not said, that the group had hoped to find in these articles?

✤ What is the overall impression of the story of the Christian faith outside the UK?

Draw together the group's findings and discuss what the group thinks about the outcome of their research. Where else might they go to find more information and stories?

What's in a word?

Different terms are used to describe our world. Can you add any more to the list below? What is positive about these terms and what is negative? Does it matter which terms we use?

✤ Third World
✤ The South
✤ The North
✤ The West
✤ Less Economically Developed Countries (LEDC)
✤ Developing Countries
✤ Poor Countries
✤ Majority World
✤ First World

CORE

What can we do about poverty?

You will need:
✳ Cards: What can we do about poverty?
(p. 75), enough for each group of three or four to have one set each

It is easy to feel powerless in the face of world poverty, especially as so many children worldwide are caught up in poverty. It is wrong to think that there is nothing we can do to change things, but we need to be wise about the help we offer.

Cut out the cards showing possible responses to poverty and put each set in a pile. Get into groups of three of four and give each group a set of cards. There should also be two blank cards in each set, so that the group can add their own responses. Ask the groups to discuss the different responses and put them into three piles: the best responses, the worst responses, and those that are in between (they might want to suggest how the responses could be improved to make them better).

Invite the groups to explain their choices. Is there any consensus on which responses to poverty are the best? How would they address any feelings of powerlessness and apathy that might come from the children they work with towards such global poverty?

Here are some discussion starters for some of the responses.

Live as simply as possible: This may seem the most self-sacrificial answer. Did any in the group put it in their 'best responses' pile or 'worst responses' pile, or was it dismissed as unrealistic?

Organise a campaign about debt or trade justice: The debt crisis is still one of the biggest causes of poverty in the world today. Poor countries give more money to rich countries in debt repayments than they receive in aid. Poor countries' share of global trade is tiny. Fair trade rules could make a huge difference to their ability to earn money.

Sponsor a child: Development agencies have different opinions on this issue. Some offer the opportunity to sponsor, write to and even visit a child in a poor country. Others believe that support for a single child may be divisive in a poor community, expensive to administer and more about meeting the needs of the donor than the needs of the child. Supporting communities to tackle poverty together is usually more effective in the long term.

There is nothing we can do: This stands out as obviously 'wrong', but many people believe it. Are there traces of this attitude hidden in what is said about other answers?

Convert everyone to Christianity: It is a historical fact that Christian countries and societies have not necessarily been fairer or less violent than non-Christian ones. Why might this be the case?

Go and show the poor how to solve their problems: How would you feel if someone from another country came and told you what your problems were and what you needed to do about it? Don't those skills exist locally?

Fight for change: Can violence end injustice? Is it ever right to use violence to achieve our goals?

Global dilemmas _____

You will need:
- ✳ 'Global dilemmas' discussion topics (p. 76), cut into five for small group work
- ✳ 'Global dilemmas' background information (p. 77)

The aim of the following exercise is to help the group think through their own views on key global issues affecting children.

The five issues to be discussed are:

- ❖ Economic migrants
- ❖ Child labour
- ❖ Generation orphan
- ❖ Child sponsorship
- ❖ Child soldiers

The facilitator of this exercise needs to prepare background information and relevant news stories on each of these issues. The organisations listed in the resources bank on the *Core Skills for Children's Work* website (www.coreskillsforchurches.com) will be a good source of information. Other useful websites on the issues include the following.

Economic migrants
World News Network:
http://economicmigrants.com

The Refugee Council:
www.refugeecouncil.org.uk

Child labour
World Education:
www.worlded.org

See also:
www.unicef.org.uk/publications/pdf/
ECECHILD2_A4.pdf

Child soldiers
Information can be found at www.warchild.org.uk.

Divide the participants into five small groups and give each group one of the 'Global dilemmas' discussion topics and the background information. Allow time for the groups to discuss the questions thoroughly and to attempt the given task. The exercise aims to draw out the complexity of some of the issues that children's leaders have to deal with and to explore the moral and ethical issues so that leaders know what they feel about these issues before they tackle them with children. The exercise

will also help the group to answer the question, 'What do you think?'

Give everyone a ten-minute and then five-minute warning to let them know when their time for discussion is coming to a close. Then invite each group to feed back to the other groups, allowing some time for discussion and comments. In particular, ask the groups to comment on:

- ❖ What they found most difficult about the exercise.
- ❖ What they have learnt.
- ❖ What they felt they needed more information about.
- ❖ How they could find out more or develop their skills in this area.

Adapted from an exercise by Paul Adams,
Development Education Association

Making connections _____

You will need:
- ✳ Case studies: Making connections (pp. 78–79)

Children in schools are encouraged to find out about other parts of the world in their studies. How might we encourage the children in our church groups to do something similar and link up with children who follow the Christian faith in other cultures or countries?

Divide into three groups and ask them to take one of the three case studies each.

- ❖ What are the advantages and disadvantages of each approach?
- ❖ In what ways might these approaches benefit the children in your own group?
- ❖ How do you think links like this might affect the faith journey of the children you know?

Spend some time sharing insights from this exercise. You could also use it as a springboard to discuss any other successful and creative ways of making links, of which group members have first-hand experience or about which they have heard.

The Bible and global issues

> You will need:
> ✳ Cards: Bible verses relating to global issues (p. 80), enough for each group to have a set

Cut out the cards and then, in small groups, pair up the global issue with the Bible passage that opens up discussion about it. Encourage the participants to look up the context for each of the key verses to facilitate a thoughtful discussion of the Bible passages.

Here is a summary of the top ten passages and an indication of the issues each one addresses.

1. Isaiah 58:1–10: God looks for social justice, not just personal righteousness.
2. Matthew 25:31–46: Our attitude to those in need is part of our response to God.
3. Psalm 104:10–15, 24–31: The interdependency of all things in God's world; environmental issues.
4. Amos 5:21–24; 8:1–6: Issues of trade justice.
5. Deuteronomy 24:19–22: Care for the vulnerable and weak.
6. Revelation 21:1–5: A just and fair world as God plans it to be.
7. Nehemiah 5:1–15: Speaking up for the poor.
8. 2 Corinthians 8:1–15: Charity and care for each other. (See also 1 Corinthians 16:1–3: Regular giving to those in need.)
9. Lamentations 2:18–20: The plight of children in need.
10. Matthew 5:6–9: Hunger for justice and hunger for peace.

For further biblical background, some or all of following passages could be included in this exercise.

✤ Micah 6:6–8: True worship
✤ Genesis 26:12–32: Issues of access to water
✤ 2 Samuel 9:1–13: Attitudes to disability
✤ Isaiah 5:1–7: A parable about social justice
✤ James 2:1–7, 14–17: Beware treating people unfairly on the grounds of wealth
✤ Deuteronomy 15:1–11: Jubilee and cancellation of debts
✤ Acts 6:1–4: Fair treatment of ethnic groups
✤ Exodus 23:1–3: A fair hearing in the law courts
✤ Exodus 23:4–9: Restraint in war and stamping out corruption
✤ Leviticus 25:39–43: Issues of slavery
✤ 2 Kings 4:1–7: Issues of famine, debt and slavery
✤ 1 Kings 21:1–29: Land rights
✤ Psalm 8:1–9: Issues of human dignity
✤ Deuteronomy 14:22–29: The principle of tithing
✤ Matthew 6:22–24: Jesus speaks about attitudes to wealth
✤ Lamentations 3:31–36: God speaks about the rights of prisoners
✤ Luke 14:12–14: Concern for the poor
✤ Proverbs 23:10–11: Land rights
✤ Deuteronomy 5:21: Curbing human greed

Enriching your programme

> You will need:
> ✳ Global voices (p. 81)

Children are global citizens too. Listen to the voices of children in the poems and quotations.

Many children have an innate passion about issues of justice and they believe that one person can make a difference.

✤ Do you agree?
✤ Is this part of their innate spirituality? If so, how can we nurture it?
✤ How can we help children do something about their passion for justice?
✤ How can we help adults in the church to hear children's voices?

To include real stories of life and faith from around the world in your work with children is one way forward. Think back over the curriculum you have been following in recent months. How often has the material included real stories from around the world? When might this have happened? What would you need to do to make it happen?

Below are some simple suggestions. There are links to resources and materials for these ideas on the Core Skills website, www.coreskillsforchurches.com.

✤ Include music and prayers from other cultures.
✤ Include pictures of Bible stories from other cultures.
✤ Include news of what is happening in other cultures in your discussion time together.
✤ Set up email links with the children of people you know who live or work in another country.
✤ Use artefacts from other countries as part of your storytelling.
✤ Include simple words of praise from other countries in your worship.
✤ Encourage and value those in your group who speak other languages, particularly when saying the Lord's Prayer together.

✤ At key festival times, find out how these festivals are celebrated by Christians in other parts of the world.

✤ Have a termly focus on supporting and sharing with a project overseas, making sure there is a balance between receiving and giving.

✤ Include worldwide issues in your prayer time together. You could perhaps always have a globe with a candle next to it to remind everyone of the worldwide perspective.

✤ Use stories and poems from around the world in your work.

✤ Invite overseas visitors to your church to spend time with the children.

✤ Get involved with a global justice issue as a group, such as writing, advocacy, action and so on.

Biblical thought

The world Church _____
Read Acts 13:1–3.

The missionary church in Antioch, which became the centre of the Christian church among the Gentiles, had a remarkably mixed leadership team. No doubt the leaders from North Africa and those from Judea would have had some different outlooks and insights to bring. Nevertheless, together they were united in prayer and God spoke clearly to them. In Acts 11:27–30 we also read how the church from Antioch responded to a request for aid from Christians in Jerusalem.

✤ How is a church enriched by hearing and acting on insights from around the Christian world?

✤ Do you think global issues might influence a church's priorities?

✤ How else might the issues affect its mission and ministry?

Read 1 Corinthians 12:12–27. In this famous passage from Paul's letter, he uses the image of a human body to describe the Church. Although the traditional application of this passage is to a local congregation and its members, it could be used in the context of the global Christian family. If Paul had been writing a letter to our church today, he might have written the following version:

For just as the body is one and has many members, so all the members of the Church, though many, are one Church. So it is with Christ. For by one Spirit we were all baptised into one Church: Europeans, Africans, Asians—all were made to drink of one Spirit.

The church in Uganda cannot say, 'Because I am not English, I do not belong to the world Church.' If the whole Church were European, where would be the unbridled enthusiasm?

There are many parts, yet one Church. The church in America cannot say to the church in Mozambique, 'I have no need of you.' Nor can the church in China say to the church in Nepal, 'I have no need of you.'

God has so blessed the Church that the members may have the same care for one another. If one part of the world Church suffers, all suffer. If one part of the world Church is honoured, all rejoice together.

You are a world Church, the body of Christ, and each one of you is a part of it.

✤ What does the group think about this version of the passage? Is it helpful or does it merely promote stereotypes?

✤ How might the group alter or add to this reading from their experience?

✤ Is it fair to extend Paul's body metaphor to the worldwide Church in this way?

Reflection on learning

Cultural expressions_____
Wherever in the world the story of the Christian faith has been taken, it has had to be 'translated' into the images and expressions that make sense within a local culture. This approach can be enormously helpful to us here and to our children, as it enables us to hear afresh some of the key facts about our faith.

Vincent Donovan tells how he re-expressed the Christian story as a creed in language and terms that made sense to the Masai people of East Africa, with whom he worked:

We believe in the one High God, who out of love created the beautiful world and everything good in it. He created man and wanted man to be happy in the world. God loves the world and every nation and tribe on the earth. We have known this High God in the darkness, and now we know him in the light. God promised in the book of his word, the Bible, that he would save the world and all the nations and tribes.

We believe that God made good his promise by sending his son, Jesus Christ, a man in the flesh, a Jew by tribe, born poor in a little village, who left his home and was always on safari doing good, curing people by the power of God, teaching about God and man, showing that the meaning of religion is love. He was rejected by his people, tortured and nailed hands and feet to a cross, and died. He lay buried in the grave, but the hyenas did not touch him, and on the third day, he rose from the grave. He ascended to the skies. He is the Lord.

We believe that all our sins are forgiven through him. All who have faith in him must be sorry for their sins, be baptised in the Holy Spirit of God, live the rules of love and share the bread together in love, to announce the good news to others until Jesus comes again. We are waiting for him. He is alive. He lives. This we believe. Amen.

Vincent J. Donovan, *Christianity Rediscovered*, p. 163

Do you have any personal experience of how Christian truths have been expressed helpfully in a language and culture other than your own? Have you found that the insights of a Christian speaker or writer from another culture have helped you understand your faith better?

Worship

You will need:

* Songs: 'If you believe and I believe' and 'He came down that we may have love' (Wild Goose Publications, www.ionabooks.com)
* *Welcome liturgy from the Church of India* (p. 82)
* *The Christ we share* or *Jesus Mafa* pictures (see page 63 for source details)
* Bible passages from page 67 or 80
* Prayers from around the world (pp. 83–84)
* 'Sharing the peace' ideas from around the world (p. 85)

Finish your session with a time of reflection and prayer, including the following items.

✤ **Songs:** Use the two songs from the worldwide Church.

✤ **Opening prayers:** Choose a selection from the Welcome liturgy from the Church of South India.

✤ **Reflection:** Place around the room six pictures from *The Christ we share*, or three copies of the paintings from *Jesus Mafa*. Invite the group to reflect on which paintings or pictures they like. Which ones do they find disturbing? Share your reflections on these images. In what ways could the different pictures of Jesus and his story help group members to come closer to God in worship?

✤ **Bible reading:** Select a passage or passages from 'The Bible and global issues' on page 67 or 80.

✤ **Prayers:** Include some prayers from around the world from pages 83–84.

✤ **Conclusion:** End by sharing the peace with each other, using one of the suggestions from other cultures and Christian communities on page 85.

Useful resources

You can find a list of useful resources and links for this module online at www.coreskillsforchurches.com/2367

Vincent J. Donovan, *Christianity Rediscovered*, SCM Press, 1982. Used by permission. Orbis Books, Maryknoll, New York, 25th anniversary edition © 2003 by Orbis Books.

1. How many people in the world don't have clean water to drink?
   a) 500 million
   b) 1.1 billion
   c) 3 billion

2. What percentage of HIV-positive people live in poor countries?
   a) 55 per cent
   b) 75 per cent
   c) 95 per cent

3. The US spends $1 billion a day on defence (about £660 million). At this rate of spending, how many days would it take to pay for health and nutrition for the whole world for one year?
   a) 13 days
   b) 120 days (about four months)
   c) 365 days (one year)

4. The three richest men in the US have more money than how many of the world's poorest people put together?
   a) 1 million
   b) 50 million
   c) 600 million

5. What percentage of deaths from natural disasters happen in developing countries?
   a) 50 per cent
   b) 63 per cent
   c) 96 per cent

6. If the world was reduced to a village of 1000 people, how many would own a computer?
   a) 1
   b) 175
   c) 460

7. A pair of boxer shorts from GAP costs £8. How much is paid to the worker who made them?
   a) £2.50
   b) £1.17
   c) 4p

8. Which country in the world hosts the most refugees?
   a) Iran
   b) Pakistan
   c) The United Kingdom

9. What percentage of global trade do poor countries have?
   a) 0.4 per cent
   b) 18 per cent
   c) 25 per cent

10. Of the 1.3 billion people living in poverty around the world, what percentage are women?
    a) 52 per cent
    b) 63 per cent
    c) 70 per cent

(See page 86 for answers.)

Children's rights and realities

The year 2009 was the 30th anniversary of the United Nations Convention on the Rights of the Child. This information sheet contains paraphrases of some extracts from that charter alongside some of the statistics about the situation for many children in our world today. The figures and percentages quoted are by necessity estimations but are based on information from UNICEF sources and from other aid agencies.

Right 2

The rights in the Convention apply to all children, whether they live in cities or towns or villages, in mountains or valleys, in deserts or forests or jungles.

✤ **Fact**: 40 per cent of the world's population is under the age of 19; there are about 1.5 billion children of primary school age; half of the people in the majority world are children.

Rights 3 and 6

We must recognise that children are precious. If they fall down, they should be picked up, and if they are lost, they should be given guidance. They should be given all they need to make them happy and strong, and we should always do our best for them when they are in our care. All children should be allowed to live and to grow until they have grown up and can decide things for themselves.

✤ **Fact**: One quarter of the world's children speak a Chinese dialect; one third of children are brought up within a Christian culture; one third of the world's children live on less than a dollar a day; one quarter do not have electricity; by the year 2100 the number of children in the world will have more than doubled.

Right 7

Every child shall have the right to a name and land to call their own.

✤ **Fact**: A large number of the world's 53 million displaced peoples are children; typically, one in 20 has lost contact with their family.

Right 9

Children have the right to be kept together with their families or, if they have no family, to be looked after and cared for with love.

✤ **Fact**: Most of the world's 'street children' are child labourers from poor urban homes. The numbers of street children are rising fast, in parallel with the rise of urban poverty. It is estimated that up to 250 million children are on the streets for various reasons—some still with regular family contact and others with only occasional family contact—and some are without homes or parents that they know about (as orphans or those who have deliberately severed ties with home for various reasons).

Right 19

Children have the right to be protected from abuse and dangers of all kinds.

✤ **Fact**: Children make up a big part of the world sex industry's workforce. It is estimated that every week, between 10 and 12 million children engage in sex for money.

Right 24

Children have the right to adequate shelter, nourishment and health care.

✤ **Fact**: Half the world's children do not have a reliable source of food and are hungry for some or all of the time; one fifth of these children are severely undernourished. A quarter of the world's children spend a large part of each day simply getting safe water and two fifths do not have adequate sanitation.

Rights 28/29

Children have the right to education so that they can grow up to be the best at whatever they wish to do. Children have the right to inherit an environment free from pollution and exploitation.

✤ **Fact**: One quarter of the world's children do not attend school and one fifth cannot read. Of those who do learn to read, they are far more likely to be boys than girls. One third of the world's children breathe air that is unhealthy because of pollution.

Reproduced with permission from *More Core Skills for Children's Work* published by BRF 2010 (978 1 84101 700 6) www.barnabasinchurches.org.uk

Right 38

Children have the right to be kept safe in times of war and not to be used as soldiers.

❖ **Fact**: It is estimated that as many as ten million children worldwide may be suffering severe trauma from witnessing genocide first-hand, from being raped, or from themselves being broken in as soldiers and sent out to kill. It is estimated that the number of child soldiers serving in the world's armies could be as many as a quarter of a million.

Sources: www.unicef.org; *If the World were a Village* (David J. Smith and Shelagh Armstrong, A&C Black, 2004); *For Every Child: the rights of the child in words and pictures* (Various authors, Red Fox, 2002); *Children in Crisis* (OM Publishing)

Maps: Seeing the world differently

Mercator project

http://upload.wikimedia.org/wikipedia/commons/thumb/7/74/Mercator-projection.jpg/773px-Mercator-projection.jpg

A standard projection of the world which, however, distorts the areas near the poles.

Peter's projection

www.wall-maps.com/World/PetersProjection-over.gif

A projection of the world that accurately reflects the land area of each continent.

New Zealand and Australia centric

http://flourish.org/upsidedownmap/hobodyer-large.jpg

A projection of the world that does not have the UK as central and 'on top'.

Projection by absolute poverty

www.worldmapper.org/display.php?selected=180

A projection of the world in which the countries with the greatest poverty are proportionally enlarged.

Absolute poverty means living on the equivalent of US$2 a day or less, to cover the basic requirements of food, shelter and water. In 2002, 43 per cent of the world's population was living on this amount.

When almost an entire population is in absolute poverty, life expectancy is short, education levels are low and there is widespread undernourishment. In both Nigeria and Mali, 90 per cent of the population survives on less than US$2 a day.

Although South America as a whole has a relatively small poor population, 39 million people in Brazil live on less than US$2 a day.

Projection by population

www.worldmapper.org/display.php?selected=2

A projection of the world in which the countries with the greatest populations are proportionally enlarged.

In Spring 2000, the population of the world reached an estimated 6 billion (6 thousand million).

India, China and Japan have large populations so they appear large on this map. Panama, Namibia and Guinea-Bissau are hardly visible because they have small populations.

Sudan, which has the largest land area in Africa, has a smaller population than Nigeria, Egypt, Ethiopia, Democratic Republic of Congo, South Africa or Tanzania.

Projection by wealth in the year 2015

www.worldmapper.org/display.php?selected=164

A projection of the world in which the countries with the greatest wealth are proportionally enlarged.

If the economic trends established between 1975 and 2002 continue until 2015, it could mean that China is producing 27 per cent of all the wealth in the world by that time.

African territories are predicted to remain small in terms of world wealth. Eastern European territories are also likely to decrease in their proportion of world wealth.

Projection by infant mortality (2002)

www.worldmapper.org/display.php?selected=261

A projection of the world in which the countries with the highest mortality rates for children are proportionally enlarged.

'Infant mortality' means babies dying during their first year of life. In 2002 there were 7.2 million infant deaths throughout the world; 5.4 per cent of all babies born alive died within their first year.

India had the highest number of infant deaths (1.7 million). In India, almost 7 per cent of babies born alive die within a year.

In 22 territories (all in Africa), the mortality rate is over 10 per cent. The highest infant mortality rate is in Sierra Leone, where 16.5 per cent of babies die within a year.

Projection by Christian faith

www.worldmapper.org/display_religion.php?selected=554

A projection of the world in which the areas with the highest numbers of Christians are proportionally enlarged.

With a total of just over 2 billion followers, Christianity is the world's biggest religion. Christians are spread widely across the world. After the Vatican City, the largest rates of Christians are found in Malta, followed by several territories in South America.

Projection by birth rate

www.worldmapper.org/display.php?selected=3

A projection of the world in which the countries with the highest birth rates are proportionally enlarged.

133,121,000 babies were born in the year 2000. More children are born each year in Africa than in the whole of Europe, the Americas and Japan put together. Worldwide, more than a third of a million people are born each day of the year.

Projection by total children

www.worldmapper.org/display.php?selected=5

A projection of the world in which the countries with the greatest number of children are proportionally enlarged.

Children make up a third of the world's population. Africa has the highest percentage: in Uganda and Niger half the population is under 15 years of age. By contrast, in Italy, Spain and Japan only 14 per cent is under the age of 15.

More maps of this sort, covering a wide range of criteria, can be found at www.worldmapper.org.

Reproduced with permission from *More Core Skills for Children's Work* published by BRF 2010 (978 1 84101 700 6) **www.barnabasinchurches.org.uk**

What can we do about poverty?

Live as simply as possible (buy less) and give the money saved to those who are poor.

Buy fairly traded goods in the supermarket.

There's nothing we can do. Human nature can't be changed!

Campaign for an increase in the overseas aid budget.

Organise a campaign to cancel the debts of poor countries or to change global trade rules.

Sponsor a child in the Third World.

Convert everyone to Christianity—it's the only way to bring about real change.

Go overseas and show the poor how to solve their problems.

Find out which countries exploit workers in the Third World and campaign for companies to adopt a code of conduct safeguarding workers' rights.

Find out about the causes of world poverty and tell others.

Raise money for local projects overseas that aim to tackle the causes of poverty and build self-reliance.

The only way to achieve change is to fight for it. Violence is the answer!

Reproduced with permission from *More Core Skills for Children's Work* published by BRF 2010 (978 1 84101 700 6) www.barnabasinchurches.org.uk

Global dilemmas discussion topics

Global dilemmas: Economic migrants

Your topic for discussion is: Who should be allowed to settle in the UK?

❖ You should aim to come up with a list of criteria.
❖ You will be given some background information that outlines some of the key issues.
❖ You should aim to present your conclusions to the whole group.

Global dilemmas: Child labour

Your topic for discussion is: Should we boycott products produced by child labour? (For the sake of this discussion, 'children' are aged 0–14.)

❖ You should be prepared to justify your opinion.
❖ You will be given some background information that outlines some of the key issues.
❖ You should aim to present your conclusions to the whole group.

Global dilemmas: Generation orphan

Your topic for discussion is: What sort of care is best for orphaned children?

❖ You should be prepared to justify your conclusions.
❖ You will be given some background information that outlines some of the key issues.
❖ You should aim to present your case to the whole group.

Global dilemmas: Child sponsorship

Your topic for discussion is: Who benefits from sponsoring a child in the developing world?

❖ You should be prepared to justify your conclusions.
❖ You will be given some background information that outlines some of the key issues.
❖ You should aim to present your case to the whole group.

Global dilemmas: Child soldiers

Your topic for discussion is: Should we campaign for an end to the arms trade?

❖ You should be prepared to justify your conclusions.
❖ You will be given some background information that outlines some of the key issues.
❖ You should aim to present your case to the whole group.

Reproduced with permission from *More Core Skills for Children's Work* published by BRF 2010 (978 1 84101 700 6) www.barnabasinchurches.org.uk

Economic migrants

For information on this issue, see the following websites:

World News Network: http://economicmigrants.com
The Refugee Council: www.refugeecouncil.org.uk

Child labour

For information on this issue, see the following websites:

www.worlded.org
www.unicef.org.uk/publications/pdf/
ECECHILD2_A4.pdf

Generation orphan

According to UNICEF, 'Orphans and vulnerable children are those unfortunate [enough] to have been deprived of their first line of protection: their parents.'

✤ Worldwide, every 15 seconds one child is orphaned by AIDS.
✤ Globally, 15.2 million children have been orphaned by AIDS, some 80 per cent living in sub-Saharan Africa.
✤ One in eight of all children in Africa have lost one or more parents.

Source: UNAIDS: *Children, the Missing Face of AIDS* (UNICEF)

For more information, go to www.unaids.org.

Related issues include child-headed households, the role of faith-based institutions, extended families, and the debate over whether it's better for vulnerable children to be housed within a home environment or in an orphanage.

Child sponsorship

Development agencies have different opinions on this issue. Some offer the opportunity to sponsor, write to and even visit a child in a poor country. Others believe that support for a single child may be divisive in a poor community, is expensive to administer and may be more about meeting the needs of the donor than the needs of the child. Supporting communities to tackle poverty together is usually more effective in the long term.

For the case for, go to World Vision:
www.worldvision.org.uk

For the case against, here is a statement from Christian Aid's website:
www.christianaid.org.uk/faqs.aspx

Christian Aid believes that it is better to help whole communities through our partner organisations rather than sponsor individuals. A village well, a community school, a trained primary health worker—these can help to improve life for everyone, rather just an individual child.

Some sponsorship schemes do support projects that benefit the community, but even then, the mechanics of sponsoring (reporting the progress of each child, translating letters, taking photos and so on) cost money. This is money being spent on the needs of the donor, not of the child.

Child soldiers

It is estimated that as many as 10 million children worldwide may be suffering severe trauma from witnessing genocide first-hand, from being raped, or from themselves being broken in as soldiers and sent out to kill. It is estimated that the number of child soldiers serving in the world's armies could be as many as a quarter of a million.

The term 'child soldier' conjures up images of gun-toting adolescent boys, but the reality is very different. A number of the world's child soldiers are actually girls—in some countries, up to 40 per cent—and many are as young as seven or eight years old.

For more information, see the following websites:

www.unicef.org.uk/publications/pub_detail.asp?
pub_id=69
www.unicef.org.uk/publications/pub_detail.asp?
pub_id=8

Case studies: Making connections

Case Study 1: Linking via the Internet

The world is on the move and, for young people in particular, there are many opportunities to travel and experience life in other parts of the globe. For Christians, there are many short-term schemes allowing them to spend time working in aid projects alongside local churches in developing countries. It is not surprising, therefore, that this has led to a number of crosscultural marriages, such as that of Sansao and Rachel Campos, who met through YWAM (Youth with a Mission) in South America. Sansao was a carpenter from a poor family in Belo Horizonte, Brazil's third largest city, and Rachel comes from the UK. Their marriage led to the founding of the Good Shepherd Project (*Projecto Bon Pastor*), which aims to bring the gospel in word and deed to many families who are caught in a vicious circle of poverty, despair and disease and who live in ramshackle shelters in the sprawling suburbs of the city.

Local churches in north-east London, where Rachel lived, soon got behind the work, learning more about it from regular email links and Internet connections. This led to the involvement of the children and young people at those churches, not only in raising money but also in finding out more about life in this part of Latin America and sharing in some of the music and stories of the life of the church there.

When the opportunity came to establish a safe house for abused and neglected children, a group of youth leaders arranged to take teams of teenagers over to South America to help decorate the house and work with the children. These summer trips proved to be significant experiences for many in the teams, some of whom have gone on to be involved in overseas work with other mission and development agencies.

Regular email links and reciprocal visits, alongside an occasional focus on the project as part of the children's programme, have continued to develop and deepen the faith of the children in the UK as well as benefiting the children in need from Belo Horizonte.

For more information on this project, go to www.goodshepherdproject.org.uk.

This is just one of many examples of links between churches in the UK and communities overseas that have sprung up in the age of email and Internet, and from relatively small beginnings. Such projects can do so much to help children catch the vision of an interdependent world and kindle their passion for making a difference as part of the mission of the church.

As a group, share stories of similar projects and links that you know about and explore the benefits and challenges of this sort of connection for children.

Case Study 2: Making connections with a shared project

Peacebuilders is a project developed by the Methodist Church, Pilots and the United Reformed Church with the Church of North India and the Henry Martyn Institute. One of the activities suggested is the creation of a peace box.

The notion of 'passing the peace' is one that is strong in Christian worship and, through *Peacebuilders*, we invite your group to physically pass the peace, in the form of a peace box, around your community. The idea is that the box will travel to different places in the community, such as schools, other churches and places of worship, libraries and shops. People will be invited to contribute their ideas about peace to the box. As the box moves on to another location, a *Peacebuilders* postcard and window sticker are left behind and can be displayed to show that the location has taken part and, in so doing, has made a commitment to peace. Your group can then see evidence of *Peacebuilders* in their local area. The box will eventually arrive back to your group and will be part of the focus for worship.

This project has been very popular. One children's worker wrote:

Our junior club created our peace box. The box spent two weeks on the church premises in our groups and other community groups. All contributed their thoughts and ideas. Now a local pottery café has our box, then it moves to our local schools. The infant school will have an assembly on peace, and the box will be in their library for a week for the children to look at and add to. Our local junior school got really excited when they heard about the project, and the box will travel to each of their classes in turn. Year 4 classes are coming to visit the church to see what we have been up to, and to start creating a peace wall.

Our local community has really taken on board the project. Local businesses are keen to have the box. A local art studio approached us

Reproduced with permission from *More Core Skills for Children's Work* published by BRF 2010 (978 1 84101 700 6) www.barnabasinchurches.org.uk

and asked if the box could visit and inspire some artwork, which I hope will form part of a display in the church. We are keen to involve the local press and may even look at the possibility of passing it to other churches with which our congregation has links.

Case Study 3: Allowing global issues to shape the curriculum

One primary school in the north-east has taken this idea wholeheartedly on board. Each half-term they plan their work based on a different country. After deciding on a country, each part of the curriculum is planned using some part of that land's geography, culture, history, language, religion and so on. Similarly, the principles of *Every Child Matters* are achieved by basing work on one particular part of the globe.

This project is attracting serious interest from curriculum planners. The guiding principles can be readily adjusted to use the idea as a planning tool for church-based groups.

Planning around *Every Child Matters*

All of what we do with children fits into one or more of these categories. This is a development from the curriculum subject grid.

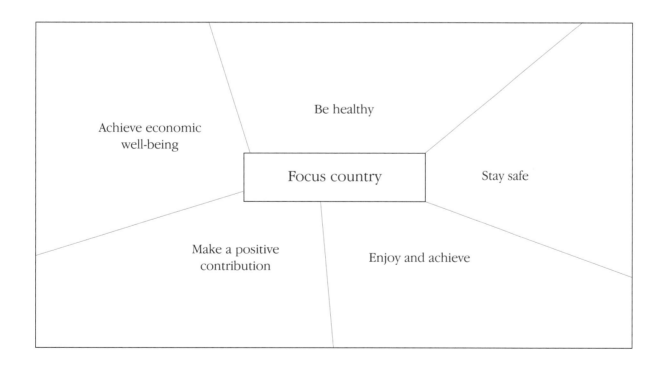

Reproduced with permission from *More Core Skills for Children's Work* published by BRF 2010 (978 1 84101 700 6) www.barnabasinchurches.org.uk

Bible stories relating to global issues

I'll tell you what it really means to worship the Lord. Isaiah 58:1–10	Issues of trade justice
God blesses those people who… Matthew 5:6–9	Our attitude to those in need is part of our response to God
Our Lord, by your wisdom you made so many things. Psalm 104:10–15 and 24–31	The plight of children in need
Don't try to get them all for yourself. Deuteronomy 24:19–22	A just and fair world as God plans it to be
I, the Lord, hate and despise your religious celebrations. Amos 5:21–24 and 8:1–6	God looks for social justice, not just personal righteousness
'Lord, when did we fail to help you?' Matthew 25:31–46	Care for each other and regular giving to those in need
When I heard their complaints… I became very angry. Nehemiah 5:1–15	Hunger for justice and for peace
And they did more than we had hoped. 2 Corinthians 8:1–15 (and 1 Corinthians 16:1–3)	The interdependency of all things in God's world: environmental issues
Now let your tears overflow. Lamentations 2:18–20	Care for the vulnerable and weak
I saw a new heaven and a new earth. Revelation 21:1–5	Speaking up for the poor

Reproduced with permission from *More Core Skills for Children's Work* published by BRF 2010 (978 1 84101 700 6) www.barnabasinchurches.org.uk

My mother's name is worry

My mother's name is worry
In summer, my mother worries about water,
In winter, she worries about coal briquettes,
And all year long, she worries about rice.

In daytime, my mother worries about living,
At night, she worries for children,
And all day long, she worries and worries.

Then my mother's name is worry,
My father's is drunken frenzy,
And mine is tears and sighs.

By a 12-year-old child in a slum area in Asia, from *Reading the Bible as Asian Women*, Christian Conference of Asia

Domingo Claudio

Domingo is ten years old and now lives at Luanda airport. He makes his living by gathering rice spilt during the unloading of food from aircraft bringing in aid. He sells the rice to market vendors.

I am my mother's eldest son. I had a little brother, but he was hit by bullets during the fighting and he died. Now I am alone. My mother was already an invalid and she was killed by rebel troops.

If you go up to someone's house, they call you a thief. And I'm not a thief. But even if you're not a thief, they accuse you of being one. Many people call us street urchins, walking the streets in dirty clothes and begging.

I think about a lot of things. I'd love to live in a house and be free. I'd like to live somewhere where I wouldn't have to fight with the others. Where I could play with friends. Where I could have a bath, wander around, watch TV. Then go to sleep and the next day play again. And after that, I'd play on the veranda with my own toys. That's what I'd like.

From *Encounters: Lost Children of Angola*, produced by Barraclough Carey for Channel 4 TV

A prayer for hungry people

Dear God,
Please help all the
Neglected people in the world
Who can't just go into the kitchen
And get a sandwich.

A child's prayer from Australia, from *Poems and Prayers for a Better World*

I wonder

I wonder what dark and gloomy creature
Took peace and unity and threw them
in the bin?
Who would want to live in a world of dark
When we can just as easily live in the light?

I wonder what would happen
If we stood by each other once in a while?
Would it make any difference,
Or would people still hover and make us fear?
I wonder.

I wonder if we ask God for forgiveness
Would he turn on the lights?
Or would he make us sit in a pit for ever?
What if we'd never made it dark in the first place?

Emily Grimes, aged 11, from *Spirited Poetry—Reflections about God, Life and Faith*, Latimer Blaylock (ed.) (RMEP, 2006)

Give us courage

Father God, some of us know
What it is to be afraid to talk to people
Of a different religion.
We are afraid because of what our
Parents will say or do to us.
We are afraid because of what our
Neighbours will say or do to us.
Give us courage.
Teach children and grown-ups in this
And every land
To show love to people
No matter what colour they are
Or by what name they are called. Amen

A child's prayer from Northern Ireland, from *Poems and Prayers for a Better World*, Su Box and Felicity Henderson (LionHudson, 2004)

A prayer for peace

Oh God, please stop people
who are fighting in wars.
Help them to see that killing people is wrong.
We pray for all children
who are in countries where there is war.
Please protect them and their families.
Help the leaders of the countries
to stop the wars
and talk together to find peace. Amen

A child's prayer, from *Poems and Prayers for a Better World*

'I wonder' from *Spirited Poetry*, reproduced with the permission of the National Association of Teachers of Religious Education

Reproduced with permission from *More Core Skills for Children's Work* published by BRF 2010 (978 1 84101 700 6) www.barnabasinchurches.org.uk

A simple welcome liturgy from the Church of India

Here is part of a service of worship from south India. A service of Christian worship in India may look rather different from the church services we are used to in the UK. Congregations normally sit on the floor and there will be the smell of incense. The service will begin with the lighting of a special lamp, which welcomes the light of Christ into the worship and reminds everyone of God's presence with his people.

A prayer to accompany the lighting of the lamp

As the light is lit, let us pray that the flame of God's living presence may spring up in our hearts and transform us by the knowledge of his glory.

Prayers of confession

Leader: Brothers and sisters, in the presence of the God of glory, we need to confess our true human condition.

In the light of Christ's self-giving life, his way of the cross, we see the darkness in our lives.

(Keep silence as we reflect on our lives as individuals)

Leader: As we think of the evil and oppression in the world of which we are a part, we need to repent together with all our brothers and sisters.

(Keep silence as we reflect on the world's life)

Leader: As members of a people called to follow Christ and live in his new righteousness, we need to repent for the evil in the Church's life.

(Keep silence as we reflect on the life of the Church)

Leader: The Saviour of the world, the refuge of the repentant, forgives and strengthens all who truly seek his grace. He accepts you as his sons and daughters and sets you free from the bondage of your past. For Christ died and rose to new life that we might all share his wholeness and abundant life. Amen

The lotus flower is very beautiful and grows even in places of dirt and squalor. In Buddhism it represents the purity of God's life that can be ours even amid the difficulties of this life. For Christians it has come to represent the new life that Christ can bring because of his resurrection from the dead. The Church of South India has combined it with the cross and adopted it as its symbol or logo.

Reproduced with permission from *More Core Skills for Children's Work* published by BRF 2010 (978 1 84101 700 6) www.barnabasinchurches.org.uk

These prayers have been selected from *A Procession of Prayers*, John Carden (ed.) (World Council of Churches, 1998).

A prayer from Bangladesh

O God, grant that always,
at all times and in all places
in all things both small and great,
we may ever do your most holy will
and be Jesus Christ's faithful servants
and handmaids to our lives' end. Amen

Used by a group of Bengali nuns, the Little Handmaids of Christ

A prayer from Egypt

O Almighty God,
help us not to give place to self-preoccupation,
which, snake-like and venomous,
winds its way so effortlessly into thought
and action;
but to take it into the desert with Christ
and to throttle it.

Based on words by Temple Gairdner of Cairo (1873–1928)

A prayer from Japan

I read
in a book
that a man called
Christ
went about doing good.
It is very disconcerting
to me
that I am so easily
satisfied
with just
going about.

Toyohiko Kagawa, Japanese social reformer (1888–1960)

A prayer from Uganda

Heavenly Father, amid all the perplexities of a changing situation, help us to learn the new ways you would have us tread; and, along every unknown path, give us the courage to follow Jesus, the same Saviour, yesterday, today and for ever.

A prayer from Croatia

God, you are the God of life.
Transform us in the depths of our hearts
into people, through whom your peace
is carried out into your world.

Send your Spirit into the hearts of those
who are captured in the net of violence,
be it as perpetrators or as victims,
and let us never give up the search
for the chance to talk to them.

A prayer from Sri Lanka

Even as the water falls on dry tea leaves
and brings out their flavour,
so may your Spirit fall on us and renew us
so that we may bring refreshment and joy
to others.

A prayer from the Orthodox Church

Come, Holy Spirit
teacher of the humble, judge of the arrogant.
Come, hope of the poor, refreshment of the weary,
rescuer of the shipwrecked.
Come, most splendid adornment
of all living beings,
the sole salvation of all who are mortal.
Come, Holy Spirit, have mercy on us,
imbue our lowliness with your power,
meet our weakness with the fullness
of your grace.
Come, Holy Spirit, renew the whole creation!

A prayer from Kenya

Almighty God, you bring to light things hidden in darkness and know the shadows of our hearts; cleanse and renew us by your Spirit that we may walk in the light and glorify your name, through Jesus Christ, the light of the world. Amen

A prayer from China

O God, grant that your Spirit may move us to enter your temple. Open our eyes that we may see your saving grace, and stretch forth our hands to receive the Lord who has come.

Reproduced with permission from *More Core Skills for Children's Work* published by BRF 2010 (978 1 84101 700 6) **www.barnabasinchurches.org.uk**

A prayer from Korea

Stay with us, Lord
for the day is far spent
and we have not yet recognised your face
in each of our brothers and sisters.

Stay with us, Lord
for the day is far spent
and we have not yet shared your bread
in grace with our brothers and sisters.

Stay with us, Lord
for the day is far spent
and we have not yet listened to your word
on the lips of our brothers and sisters.

Stay with us, Lord
because our very night becomes day
when you are there.

Reproduced with permission from *More Core Skills for Children's Work* published by BRF 2010 (978 1 84101 700 6) www.barnabasinchurches.org.uk

The peace of Christ is passed between worshippers in services all around the globe. In different cultures and traditions, though, there are a variety of ways in which it is done.

In Africa

Stand people in a circle or circles. The leader who starts the sharing of the peace (A) turns to the person on his or her left (B) and shakes hands, while at the same time turning that person so that they change places. The person who started (A) does the same again with the new person to his or her left (C), so that they too change places. When these two movements are complete, (B) can turn to the person on his or her left and start the process. Soon there will be lots of circling handshakes happening all round the circle and the dance of peace continues until it has passed round the whole circle and everyone is back in their original positions.

To add further flavour, you could try to make the handshake particularly African. This involves first a normal handshake, then a linking of the thumbs while the rest of the hand clasps the other at an angle, then back to a normal handshake, then thumbs, then handshake and then thumbs again. Different parts of Africa have different traditions about how many times this is done.

In Orthodox worship

The first person puts their hands together, as if in a prayer position, around the hands of another, also in a prayer position. In this way it is as if the peace surrounds the hands of those who receive it and is then passed on.

Among the Maasai of East Africa

To the Maasai, a tuft of green grass is very sacred. It means food for their cattle and is also a sign that precious water must be nearby. To exchange a tuft of grass with another is a sign of peace and an assurance that there will be no more violence between those involved. The Maasai pass green grass in their Communion services as a sign of the peace of Christ. In the tribe's rewording of the Sermon on the Mount, heaven is referred to as 'the green pastures of God'.

In Swahili

The words for 'The peace of the Lord be with you' are *Mungu akubaribe*.

In Romanian

The words 'The peace of the Lord be with you' are accompanied by an embrace to the right and then to the left. The words are *Pace Domnului* (pronounced 'pachay dom-noo-looey').

Reproduced with permission from *More Core Skills for Children's Work* published by BRF 2010 (978 1 84101 700 6) www.barnabasinchurches.org.uk

Global issues quiz: Answers

1. b) 1.1 billion
2. b) 75 per cent
3. a) 13 days
4. c) 600 million
5. c) 96 per cent
6. a) 1
7. c) 4p
8. b) Pakistan
9. a) 0.4 per cent
10. c) 70 per cent

Personal reflection sheet

What did you learn from this session?

How will this affect the way you work with children?

What further items in this area would you like to follow up?

Reproduced with permission from *More Core Skills for Children's Work* published by BRF 2010 (978 1 84101 700 6) www.barnabasinchurches.org.uk

Portfolio checklist

Learning outcomes

❖ To have an increased understanding of the ways in which the Christian faith is expressed and experienced around the world.

❖ To explore insights from other cultures and other perspectives on life and faith.

❖ To review the cultural content of current materials and practice and consider possible changes.

❖ To be more aware of the challenges and complexities of the global issues affecting children.

❖ To consider ways in which children can be involved in the Christian mission to care for and be engaged with God's world.

❖ To reflect on some Bible passages that relate to global issues.

To show that the learning outcomes have been achieved, your portfolio must include at least the following. *(Tick when you have included each one in the file.)*

☐ Personal reflection sheet

☐ Notes on the different sorts of maps

☐ Your thoughts on considering global dilemmas with children

☐ Your own thoughts on one of the global dilemmas

☐ Ways you might enlarge the global dimension of the work you do with children

☐ A response to one of the Bible passages in this module

☐ Any other responses or reflections you wish to include

The participant's involvement in a group for More Core Session 4, 'The Global Dimension', is confirmed. The learning outcomes have been evidenced through the portfolio provided.

Signed (assessor) _____ Date _____

Any comments from assessor

Signed (candidate) _____ Date _____

Reproduced with permission from *More Core Skills for Children's Work* published by BRF 2010 (978 1 84101 700 6) www.barnabasinchurches.org.uk

MORE CORE SESSION FIVE
Children's advocacy

Aims

To explore the role of advocacy in children's work; to explore the balance between advocating for the child and enabling the child's own voice to be heard; to question the role of the Children's Advocate.

Learning outcomes

* ❖ To understand what we mean by advocacy.
* ❖ To explore different models of advocacy and discuss them in relation to what we can achieve within our role as children's workers.
* ❖ To explore our own attitudes towards children and advocacy roles.
* ❖ To understand the role of local schools councils (the child advocate).
* ❖ To explore what could prevent children from being heard.
* ❖ To ensure that children feature in the general work of the church.
* ❖ To advocate the importance of children's, youth and family work in the church and wider community.

Materials needed

Starters

* ✳ A piece of paper with a body outline on it for each member of the group
* ✳ Felt-tipped pens, pencils or coloured crayons
* ✳ 'Definitions of advocacy' sheet (page 94)
* ✳ Flip chart
* ✳ Access to the website www.dcsf.gov.uk/everychildmatters/ (optional)

CORE

* ✳ Sample case studies (pages 95–96)
* ✳ Access to the website www.methodistchildren.org.uk/yearofthechild.htm (optional)
* ✳ Access to the website www.oco.ie (optional)
* ✳ Attitude statements (page 97)
* ✳ Either empty cardboard boxes and thick felt-tipped pens or Post-it notes and building blocks or bricks
* ✳ Postcards and felt-tipped pens (optional)
* ✳ 'Top ten tips' list (page 98)
* ✳ Paper and pens

Biblical thought

* ✳ Bibles for each person in the group
* ✳ Charter for children in the church (page 99)

Reflection on learning

✻ Personal reflection sheets
✻ Pens or pencils

Worship

✻ Reflective music
✻ 'Design a child' pictures (see page 91)
✻ Copies of the URC's *Charter for children in the church* (page 99), with the ten statements cut into separate strips

Opening thought

Janusz Korczak was one of the world's first advocates of children's rights. He founded the first national children's newspaper and testified on behalf of children in the early juvenile courts. He was and is known as 'The king of children'.

Children are not the people of tomorrow, but people today. They are entitled to be taken seriously. They have a right to be treated by adults with tenderness and respect, as equals, not as masters and slaves. They should be allowed to grow into whoever they were meant to be: the unknown person inside each of them is the hope for the future.
Janusz Korczak, quoted in Betty Jean Lifton, *The King of Children* (Chatto & Windus, 1988)

Starters

Design a child

> You will need:
> * A piece of paper with a body outline on it for each member of the group
> * Felt-tipped pens, pencils or coloured crayons

Putting a child at the forefront of our thinking helps us to relate to the session on a personal level. Give each group member a piece of paper with a body outline on it. Ask each one to think of a child whom they work with or know, and to depict that child on the piece of paper. (This can be done through illustration or words, but remember to protect identities.) Encourage them to include information such as what type of family the child is from, what his or her characteristics are and the situation in which the child lives. When the exercise has been completed, invite the group members to talk about their children with each other.

After the discussion, stick the pictures of the children up somewhere where they can be seen easily. Throughout the rest of the session, relate thoughts and discussions back to these children and consider the impact upon them as known individuals.

NB: It is best if the child pictures are placed at eye level to the group rather than on the floor.

What is an advocate?

> You will need:
> * 'Definitions of advocacy' sheet (p. 94)
> * Flip chart

The term 'advocate' can be traced back to the 14th century (from Latin *advocatus*, past participle of *advocare*, 'to summon': circa 1340).

As a group, explore different definitions of advocacy and talk about which ones resonate with us today. Discuss what comes to mind when you hear the word 'advocate' and record the answers on to a flip chart .

Distribute the 'Definitions of advocacy' sheet and, in small groups, discuss which definitions best agree with your own work with children. Using ideas from the examples given, or using your own ideas, try to define your role as an advocate. Share the results with the group.

NB: There are two types of advocacy: advocacy on behalf on someone else and advocacy for oneself (self-advocacy).

Advocacy through time

> You will need:
> * (Optional) Access to the website www.dcsf.gov.uk/everychildmatters/

Following the work on definitions of advocacy, explore what it means today in light of our understanding of children. For example, see The United Nations Convention on the Rights of the Child (see www.dcsf.gov.uk/everychildmatters for more information).

Discuss how the term 'advocacy' may have been used in relation to children over time and what it means within children's work today. Are we speaking for those who cannot speak? Explore what advocacy may mean for the children identified in the 'Design a child' exercise.

CORE

Models of advocacy

> You will need:
> * Sample case studies (pp. 95–96)
> * Access to the website www.methodistchildren.org.uk/ yearofthechild.htm (optional)
> * Access to the website www.oco.ie (optional)

Explore different models of advocacy and discuss them in relation to what we can achieve within our role as children's workers. First of all, distribute the sample case studies and encourage the group to read them all and discuss their opinions on each one.

* What lessons can be learnt from the case studies?
* Is there anything in them that could be replicated in situations known to us?
* What different roles are the adults fulfilling in each scenario?
* What examples can be added by the group?

Attitudes

> You will need:
> * Attitude statements (p. 97)

Use the attitude statements to encourage discussion. Read each statement aloud and ask the group to go to different parts of the room to show whether they agree, disagree or can't decide about each attitude. Encourage discussion and constructive challenge as the activity begins. Always remember the golden rule: 'Challenge the comment, not the person.'

Stumbling blocks

> You will need:
> * Either empty cardboard boxes and thick felt-tipped pens or Post-it notes and building blocks or bricks
> * Postcards and felt-tipped pens (optional)

Having decided that advocacy is about ensuring that the voice of the child is heard, either directly or indirectly, as a group look at the barriers in our churches that could prevent us from hearing that voice.

Make available a number of empty cardboard boxes. Give each person a thick felt-tipped pen and encourage them to write one barrier on each box, or on stickers on building blocks or bricks.

When everyone has completed the exercise, create a giant graffiti wall and invite the group members to sit on either side of the wall. Play a short game of charades. How easy is it to understand what is going on when a wall is dividing the group? Group members could take individual blocks home with them as a reminder of issues that they are going to address in their own church.

Alternatively, place the 'Design a child' outlines created earlier (see page 91) on the table or floor. Ask each person to write a barrier on a postcard and place the cards on top of the child outlines.

Once everyone has had a chance to write down their ideas, explore what has been written, noticing any 'groups' of barriers. Having identified these barriers, as a group explore what we can do to remove them and enable the voice of the child to be heard. Discuss what we can achieve realistically in our roles and what issues the whole church needs to address.

Ten top tips

> You will need:
> * 'Top ten tips' list (p. 98)

In light of all the discussions during the sessions and your work in small groups, create a list of 'Top ten tips' for adults on the subject of advocacy. If they are needed, you could distribute the examples given on page 98.

Skills and knowledge

> You will need:
> * Paper and pens

In small groups, design a job description showing which skills and knowledge are needed to fulfil the role of a youth and children's work advocate. Remembering that each person in the group will bring their own gifts and knowledge to the role, encourage people to be creative in the way they perceive that the role needs to be fulfilled.

Essential tasks might include:

* To advocate the importance of children's, youth and family work in the church and wider community.
* To develop and maintain a local contact list.
* To hold an overview, with others, of the activity and awareness of all youth and children's work in your area.
* To promote and support youth, children's and family events in your area and, where possible, the wider church.
* To relate to other advocates through informal structures.
* To support the local work through prayer.
* To share good news and good practice stories locally and across the wider church.

Encourage the group to reflect on which skills they already possess, as individuals, and in which areas they might need more development or training.

Biblical thought

> You will need:
> * Bibles for each person in the group
> * Charter for children in the church (p. 99)

The following study is based on the *Charter for children in the church* from the United Reformed Church.

Charter for children in the church
1. Children are equal partners with adults in the life of the church.
2. The full diet of Christian worship is for children as well as adults.
3. Learning is for the whole church, adults and children.
4. Fellowship is for all—each belonging meaningfully to the rest.
5. Service is for children to give, as well as adults.
6. The call to evangelism comes to all God's people of whatever age.
7. The Holy Spirit speaks powerfully through children as well as adults.
8. The discovery and development of gifts in children and adults is a key function of the church.
9. As a church community we must learn to do only those things in separate age groups which we cannot in all conscience do together.
10. The concept of the 'priesthood of all believers' includes children.

Read out the *Charter for children in the church*. Then ask individuals within the group to look up the following Bible passages and read them out aloud to the whole group.

1. Children are equal partners: Acts 2:39
2. The full diet of worship is for children: Psalm 148:11–12
3. Learning is for the whole church: Acts 18:8
4. Fellowship is for all: Acts 21:5–6
5. Service is for children: John 6:9
6. The call to evangelism comes to all: 2 Kings 5:2–3
7. The Holy Spirit speaks through children: 1 Samuel 3:10
8. The discovery and development of gifts: 1 Samuel 16:18
9. Do nothing separately that can't be done together: Luke 2:46–47
10. 'Priesthood of all believers' includes children: Mark 9:36–37

If time is short, focus on the following passages: Acts 2:39; Luke 2:46–47; Mark 9:36–37; Psalm 148:11–12.

Reflection on learning

> You will need:
> * Personal reflection sheet printed out (one per person)
> * Pens or pencils

Using the Personal reflection sheet, draw out action points for yourself in your ongoing work with children.

Worship

> You will need:
> * Reflective music
> * The 'Design a child' pictures
> * Copies of the URC's *Charter for children in the church* (p. 99), with the ten statements cut into separate strips

Sit the group in a circle. Place the 'Design a child' pictures in the centre of the circle. Read out the URC's *Charter for children in the church*. During a time of musical reflection, invite people to take one of the ten statements from the *Charter for children in the church* and place it on their own picture. Encourage them to think about which statement most reflects the need of the individual child they have in mind.

Useful resources

* UN Rights of the Child
* *Will You Make a Difference?* DVD from CGMC & Children Matter

Dictionary definitions

To advocate (verb): To publicly support or suggest an idea, development or way of doing something (Cambridge dictionary)

An advocate (noun): One that pleads the cause of another; specifically: one that pleads the cause of another before a tribunal or judicial court; one that defends or maintains a cause or proposal; one that supports or promotes the interests of another (Merriam Webster dictionary)

Advocate (noun and verb): An intercessor or defender; to plead in favour of; to recommend (Chambers dictionary)

Synonyms

Supporter, promoter, backer, believer, activist, campaigner, sponsor, encourager, mediator, go-between, arbitrator, intermediary, herald, spokesperson, representative, speaker, voice, negotiator, referee.

Bible references

Each of the following references has been quoted in two different Bible translations. You may wish to carry out research with other translations to tease out the definition of advocacy even further.

Job 16:19
- Even now my witness is in heaven; my advocate is on high (NIV).
- Even now, God in heaven is both my witness and my protector (CEV).

Job 16:20–21
- My intercessor is my friend as my eyes pour out tears to God; on behalf of a man he pleads with God as a man pleads for his friends (NIV).
- My friends have rejected me, but God is the one I beg to show that I am right, just as a friend should (CEV).

Romans 8:26
- In the same way, the Spirit helps us in our weakness. We do not know what we ought to pray for, but the Spirit himself intercedes for us with groans that words cannot express (NIV).
- In certain ways we are weak, but the Spirit is here to help us. For example, when we don't know what to pray for, the Spirit prays for us in ways that cannot be put into words (CEV).

1 John 2:1
- My dear children, I write this to you so that you will not sin. But if anybody does sin, we have one who speaks to the Father in our defence—Jesus Christ, the Righteous One (NIV).
- My children, I am writing this so that you won't sin. But if you do sin, Jesus Christ always does the right thing, and he will speak to the Father for us (CEV).

The first duty of a wise advocate is to convince his opponents that he understands their arguments, and sympathises with their just feelings.

Samuel Taylor Coleridge

The local church youth council: advocating the children's voices

A local church employed a youth worker to coordinate the main work of the church with children and young people. The worker quickly realised that the children were disengaged with the wider work of the church, especially concerning the management of the church and its activities. The children were not consulted on anything, including their own programmes, and did not have representation in the groups that planned these programmes.

The worker set up a group that all the children were able to attend, which would meet regularly to look at what the adult church members were discussing in AGMs and the curriculum planned for the children's own groups. The worker helped the children understand the subjects and facilitated discussions and creative sessions, enabling the children to voice their feelings, opinions, concerns and ideas. The worker then took these comments back into the wider church through the AGM and planning meetings. Where possible, she would use the children's actual words and phrases and sometimes showed video soundbites of them talking.

The long-term plan is to give the children the communication skills they need to be able to present their message, and to work with the church to make AGMs more accessible to children. The aim is to enable children to represent themselves to the wider church.

Church of Scotland

In the year 2000, the Church of Scotland decided to launch a process to enable children to have their voices heard in the national and local church. The process was called 'Year of the Child', and at its heart were children's forums. These were local groups that met over a two-year period and discussed a huge variety of issues, which they then reported back to the local and the national church.

An initial training pack was sent to each church, with advice and suggestions on how the forums should be run and how to encourage children to be part of the forums. Every six to eight weeks, a new agenda was sent to each forum leader to stimulate more discussion. The agendas formed a structured profile across the life of the church.

After the process was finished, a representative group of the children's forums attended the General Assembly of the Church of Scotland. At this assembly, a vision statement regarding children in the Church of Scotland was adopted.

To learn more about the forums and to view the agendas and training pack, visit the website: www.methodistchildren.org.uk/yearofthechild.htm

Local school councils: the child advocate

School councils have been around for about 40 years, but now, with Citizenship again being taught as part of the PSHE curriculum, many more have been established.

A school council is a group of students who are elected to represent the views of all pupils and to improve their school. There is usually a good representation of all the year groups. The term 'school council' can refer to all kinds of school-based groups run by students, including student forums and youth parliaments.

A school council does a number of things. The council meets (usually with a teacher present) to discuss and, where possible, resolve problems. These may include school lunch menus, behaviour problems or ideas for fundraising events. Members of the school council will be responsible for carrying out the ideas that have been agreed, such as planning discos, writing newspaper articles or meeting with catering staff. The teaching staff representative will have to do likewise in reporting back to the staff team.

Many schools have councils but they are not all successful. These are some factors that make a council effective:

- Regular meetings
- A council that is not too big
- Class and form councils that meet regularly
- Good communication between representatives and their class
- Training for school council members
- Smaller groups (subcommittees) working on specific events or issues
- A bank account or budget (however small)
- Annual evaluations

Reproduced with permission from *More Core Skills for Children's Work* published by BRF 2010 (978 1 84101 700 6) www.barnabasinchurches.org.uk

British and Irish Network of Ombudsmen and Children's Commissioners

In England, Scotland, Wales and Northern Ireland there are Children's Commissioners, and there is an Ombudsman for Children in the Republic of Ireland. Their key role is to represent the views or concerns of children in a variety of ways. They also feed in to and interpret government policy with regard to children and they often work on behalf of children's welfare. Visit their websites for information about their work and how it can affect you locally (see www.oco.ie for further details).

Attitude statements

- Children will always need someone willing to speak for them.

- Children under the age of 6 cannot be advocates for themselves.

- Those who are working with the children make the best advocates.

- You need to be a strong person to be an advocate.

- The church will never see children as a priority if they do not speak up for themselves.

- The term 'child advocate' is the latest 'fashion' and is tokenistic.

- The leadership of the church should meet regularly with all its stakeholders, and this includes the children.

- The Bible reminds us that God is found in the 'still small voice'.

- Children should be invited to church business meetings.

- A church that is not listening to its children will not survive.

- If a church wants to be relevant, it needs to let the children take the lead.

- Children should be practically involved in every aspect of church.

- A church cannot be described as child-friendly if the children have no voice.

- If we listened to the children more, we would see their families attending also.

- Children want to be listened to and consulted.

Reproduced with permission from *More Core Skills for Children's Work* published by BRF 2010 (978 1 84101 700 6) www.barnabasinchurches.org.uk

Top ten tips

1. Ensure that children feature in the general work of the church. Include a question about children in every church meeting agenda item: 'How will this decision impact on the children in this church?'

2. Speak to the children in your church about any big changes coming up—for example, family services, change of minister, building projects and so on.

3. Create an atmosphere in which children know that they are listened to and have the right to voice their opinion.

4. Always feed back to the children after consultation to explain what has happened as a result of their comments.

5. Give older children and young people training and support in developing skills to use in self-advocation—for example, communication skills.

6. Model good practice in listening to children by regularly evaluating the work you do with children.

7. Explore ways to enable and encourage involvement of very young children in consultation, such as the use of simple questions and methods for feedback—for example, 'What is it that makes this church a happy place?'

8. Give each child a camera and ask them to take pictures of things that make the church a happy place, or simply walk them around the church and write down the answers they tell you.

9. Notice those in the group who are natural advocates and make a start with them. Involve children in the planning of their programmes.

10. Encourage the church to do things together as a whole family. This will help with relationships and improve levels of understanding with each other.

Reproduced with permission from *More Core Skills for Children's Work* published by BRF 2010 (978 1 84101 700 6) www.barnabasinchurches.org.uk

Charter for children in the church

1. Children are equal partners with adults in the life of the church.

2. The full diet of Christian worship is for children as well as adults.

3. Learning is for the whole church, adults and children.

4. Fellowship is for all—each belonging meaningfully to the rest.

5. Service is for children to give, as well as adults.

6. The call to evangelism comes to all God's people of whatever age.

7. The Holy Spirit speaks powerfully through children as well as adults.

8. The discovery and development of gifts in children and adults is a key function of the church.

9. As a church community we must learn to do only those things in separate age groups which we cannot in all conscience do together.

10. The concept of the 'priesthood of all believers' includes children.

Reproduced with permission from *More Core Skills for Children's Work* published by BRF 2010 (978 1 84101 700 6) www.barnabasinchurches.org.uk

Personal reflection sheet

What did you learn from this session?

```



```

How will this affect the way you work with children?

```



```

What further items in this area would you like to follow up?

```



```

Portfolio checklist

Learning outcomes

❖ To understand what we mean by advocacy.

❖ To explore different models of advocacy and discuss them in relation to what we can achieve within our role as children's workers.

❖ To explore our own attitudes towards children and advocacy roles.

❖ To understand the role of local schools councils (the child advocate).

❖ To explore what could prevent children from being heard.

❖ To ensure that children feature in the general work of the church.

❖ To advocate the importance of children's, youth and family work in the church and wider community.

To show that the learning outcomes have been achieved, your portfolio must include at least the following. *(Tick when you have included each one in the file.)*

☐ Personal reflection sheet

☐ 'Design a child' picture

☐ Personal reflections on definitions of advocacy

☐ Personal response to the 'models of advocacy' questions

☐ Personal responses to 'stumbling blocks' or reflections on what you could do to remove barriers and enable the voice of the child to be heard

☐ Youth and children's work advocate job description

☐ Any other responses or reflections you wish to include

The participant's involvement in a group for More Core Session 5, 'Children's Advocacy', is confirmed. The learning outcomes have been achieved through the evidence provided.

Signed (assessor) _____ Date _____

Any comments from assessor

Signed (candidate) _____ Date _____

MORE CORE SESSION SIX
Young leaders

Aim

To focus on issues specific to young leaders in the 14–18 age group, emphasising their unique and valuable contribution to any leadership team, encouraging reflection and developing practical skills.

Learning outcomes

❖ To develop an understanding of expectations placed upon young leaders by the children, by other leaders and by themselves.
❖ To recognise and affirm the unique contribution that young leaders can make to a leadership team working with children.
❖ To become aware of a range of leadership styles and understand some of the factors that may influence our approach to leadership.
❖ To understand how young leaders can relate to children in a safe and appropriate manner.
❖ To develop more effective communication between young leaders and children.
❖ To understand the value of reflection upon the practice of leadership, both their own and their co-workers'.
❖ To reflect on their own faith journey and how it influences their work with children.

Materials needed

Starters

✳ Post-it notes
✳ A box of long matches
✳ A bowl of water or sand
✳ A flipchart and marker pens
✳ Paper and pens

Core

✳ Copies of the 'Advert for a children's worker' (page 112)
✳ Copies of the 'Outline of a child' (page 113)
✳ A sign for each station (3–5s, 5–7s, 7–11s), ideally including a picture of a child in that age group
✳ Copies of the 'Common characteristics of children' lists, cut into strips (pages 114–116)
✳ Sticky tack
✳ Paper and pens
✳ Flip chart paper and marker pens

Biblical thought

✳ Copies of the 'Leadership style' cards, cut out (page 117)
✳ Bibles
✳ Paper and pens
✳ Flipchart and marker pens

Reflection on learning

* Flip chart
* Paper and pens
* Copies of the 'What would you do if…?' scenarios (page 118)
* An adult translation of the Bible and a children's translation (such as the *International Children's Bible*)

Worship

* A selection of resources to help create an act of worship (see page 110)
* A Bible
* Bowls and towels
* A picture of Jesus washing Peter's feet
* Scissors, pens, glue
* Copies of the people outline, hexagons or cube net (pages 119–121)
* Music
* Wallpaper lining roll
* Post-it notes
* Pens

Opening thought

Don't let anyone make fun of you, just because you are young. Set an example for other followers by what you say and do, as well as by your love, faith, and purity.

1 Timothy 4:12

Starters

Famous leaders

> **You will need:**
> ✽ Post-it notes with the name of a well-known leader written on each one, enough for the group to have one each

Give out the Post-it notes showing the names of well-known leaders (but describe them as 'well-known people' rather than 'well-known leaders'). Each group member sticks their Post-it note on their forehead without looking at the name. Everyone then asks questions of each other in order to identify the name of their person. These questions must only be answered with 'Yes', 'No' or 'Don't know'.

To finish the activity, ask everyone in turn to name their person, and invite participants to suggest what all of these people have in common. Draw out the point that they are (or were) all famous leaders.

Inspiring leaders

> **You will need:**
> ✽ A box of long matches

Ask each participant to think of a Christian leader who has inspired them personally and to reflect on what made that leader so inspiring. For each person in turn, light a match and allow that person the time it takes for the match to burn down (20–30 seconds) to talk to the rest of the group about the inspiring leader. Draw out from these examples some of the qualities of a good leader.

NB: To ensure that spent matches are fully extinguished, place them in a bowl of water or sand before disposal.

Changing places

> **You will need:**
> ✽ A flip chart and marker pens
> ✽ Paper and pens

On a flip chart, write the following questions about the transition into a leadership role. Ask everyone to get into pairs or small groups and discuss the questions. If possible, mix up those who are already leading with those who have not yet started.

❖ For those who have not yet started in their role as young leaders:
  - What are you looking forward to?
  - What are you nervous about?
  - What do you hope to achieve?
  - How do you think your new role will change the way you behave?
  - How do you think it will change your relationship with the adult leaders?
  - How do you think it will change your relationship with the children?

❖ For those who are already involved as young leaders:
  - What are you enjoying?
  - What has surprised you?
  - How has your leadership role changed the way you behave?
  - How has it changed your relationship with the adult leaders?
  - How has it changed your relationship with the children?
  - What do you find difficult?

Feed back to the whole group, and draw out some of the key changes that take place in the transition to leadership.

CORE

Quality leaders needed

> **You will need:**
> ✽ Copies of the advert for a children's worker (p. 112)
> ✽ Paper and pens

Divide into small groups of three or four. Using the advert outline, invite each small group to write an advert to recruit a new children's leader. In their advert they can use no more than five of the qualities listed below, so they need to prioritise the most important.

❖ Safe person to work with children
❖ Reliable
❖ Sets a good example to children
❖ Motivated by love for the children
❖ Loves God
❖ Good at getting to know children
❖ Has creative craft ideas

- ♣ Knows their own strengths and limitations
- ♣ A good team player
- ♣ Shouts loudly
- ♣ Plans and prepares in advance
- ♣ Learns from mistakes
- ♣ Wants to keep on learning and growing
- ♣ Great at sports
- ♣ Good-looking
- ♣ Young
- ♣ Old

Once the groups have finished their adverts and read them out to the larger group, ask the participants why they chose those five qualities. Were there any others they would have included, that weren't on the list? Talk through the qualities that are necessary. Many jobs now have a 'Person Specification' attached to them, with lists of 'essential' and 'desirable' qualities. Which of the above qualities would you put in the 'essential' list for a children's worker?

Knowing me, knowing you

> **You will need:**
> ✲ Copies of the 'Outline of a child' (p. 113)
> ✲ A sign for each station (3–5, 5–7, 7–11), ideally including a picture of a child in the relevant age group
> ✲ Copies of the 'Common characteristics of children' lists, cut into strips (pp. 114–116)
> ✲ Sticky tack
> ✲ Pens

It is really important to understand the stages of development that children go through and the implications of those stages for the way in which we work with children at different ages.

Exercise 1
Give each group member a copy of the 'Outline of a child'. Ask them to think of a particular child, known to them, and fill in as much information about the child as they can on the outline. Use the following questions as a guide.

- ♣ What's their favourite game?
- ♣ What makes them laugh?
- ♣ Can they read yet?
- ♣ Who do they live with?
- ♣ Are they quiet or loud?
- ♣ What do they most enjoy doing?

Encourage participants to keep the outline over the next few weeks and see what more they can add about their chosen child. In their own time, if possible, participants should repeat this exercise with reference to other children.

Exercise 2
Around the room set up three stations, one marked '3–5 years', one marked '5–7 years' and one marked '7–11 years'. Photocopy and cut up the lists of characteristics, without the age groupings, and place them all in the middle of the room. Give the group ten minutes to allocate the statements to the appropriate stations.

Talk about each age group, highlighting some of the main characteristics for that group and asking the question, 'So what does this mean for the way I work with children of this age?' For example, the fact that children aged 5–7 respond to the hero in a story makes this a good age for using Bible stories about people who did great things for God. Similarly, the fact that children aged 3–7 learn best through physical activity means that we need to provide activities for them that involve moving about.

Working together

> **You will need:**
> • Paper and pens

There is no one person who has all the necessary gifts and skills to do everything necessary to run a good children's group. That's why it's so important that we work in teams.

Exercise 1
Give everyone in the group a piece of blank paper and ask them to write their name at the bottom of the page. Sitting in a circle, pass the papers clockwise. Everyone writes something affirming about the person whose name is on the sheet, specifically about their gifts and skills. Then fold the paper over (as in the game of Consequences) and pass it on to the next person. Repeat until everyone has written on all the papers. Every group member should then receive their own paper back.

Take a few moments to read what people have written. If they wish, participants can simply say what they think their gifts are.

> **Trainer's note**
> Refer to CORE Skills Session 2 for more on the theme of teamwork. The section about Belbin, in particular, would link well with this exercise.

Exercise 2

In small groups, discuss the following two questions. If necessary, form a group for adult leaders with rephrased questions.

❖ What can you offer, as a young leader, that adult leaders can't offer or would find difficult?
❖ What can adult leaders offer that you, as a young leader, can't offer or would find difficult?

Take a short time to feed back, drawing out the point that we each bring qualities to the team that others do not have.

Exercise 3

Sometimes teams do not work well together. Three of the main reasons why teams don't work are:

❖ Lack of trust between team members
❖ Differing aims for the group
❖ Uncertainty among individuals about their role in the team

Discuss how a team might work to overcome or avoid these issues.

> **Trainer's note**
> For more on this, see Patrick Lencioni, *The Five Dysfunctions of a Team*, Jossey Bass, 2002.

Great expectations

> **You will need:**
> ✳ Flip chart paper and marker pens

Different people (adult leaders, young leaders themselves and children in the group) may have quite different expectations of a young leader. Place three large pieces of paper on the floor with one of the following groups written on each:

❖ Children
❖ Adult leaders
❖ Yourself

Ask the participants to suggest and write on to each piece of paper what that group may expect from a young leader. Once finished, identify any similarities and differences.

Discuss what can reasonably be expected of a young leader. For example:

❖ Keeping confidentiality of information shared at leaders' meetings

❖ Preparing well
❖ Trying their best (and failing, like everyone else!)
❖ Letting the team leader know if they're unable to be at a meeting or group session

Discuss what might be unreasonable expectations of a young leader. For example:

❖ Not making mistakes
❖ Working without an adult leader present. (Young leaders under 18 cannot take legal responsibility *in loco parentis* and must be counted as children in the adult-to-child ratio)
❖ Sole responsibility for keeping official records, including attendance, financial and legal documents
❖ Walking children home (unless the parent has authorised the young leader for this role by name and in writing)
❖ Administering first aid
❖ Dealing with more serious discipline issues
❖ Contacting parents about issues involving their children

When you have identified the expectations, consider writing them up as a booklet to be given to each team member—both young leaders and adult leaders—or incorporate them into job descriptions.

Biblical thought

Jesus' styles of leadership

> **You will need:**
> ✳ Copies of the 'Leadership style' cards, cut out (p. 117)
> ✳ Bibles
> ✳ Paper and pens
> ✳ Flip chart

Within both Christian and secular circles, Jesus is considered to be one of the greatest leaders. He adapted his leadership style to the needs of different situations and people. Some of these leadership styles are:

❖ Descriptive style: the 'Do it the way I tell you' leader who closely controls people. (Although this sounds harsh, it may sometimes be an appropriate style for a particular situation.)
❖ Achievement style: the 'Firm but fair' leader who gives people clear direction and encourages by persuasion and feedback on task performance.

- Personal style: the 'People first, task second' leader who emphasises personal relationships in the organisation and stimulates people by trying to keep them happy with fringe benefits, security, social activities and a comfortable atmosphere.
- Democratic style: the 'One person, one vote' leader who encourages people's input in decision-making and recognises and rewards team effort.
- Pace-setting style: the 'Do it myself' leader who performs many tasks personally, expects members to follow his or her example and challenges by setting high standards and letting people work on their own.
- Mentor style: the 'You can do it' leader who helps and encourages members to improve their performance and encourages by providing opportunities for personal development.

Share observations and questions about these styles.

Show the group the 'Leadership style' cards, each of which shows one of the leadership styles that Jesus demonstrated. Split the groups into twos or threes and ask each small group to look at one or two of the Bible passages listed below, in which Jesus demonstrates or teaches about leadership. (Don't give away the suggested 'answers' at this stage.)

Each small group should read the passage and discuss which style of leadership is being used by Jesus and why they think it appropriate in that situation. Invite each small group to feed back and list the styles on a flip chart. Ask participants to give examples of times when they themselves have employed that style of leadership or when they have seen it employed by someone else. Consider whether it was the most appropriate or effective style for the situation.

Matthew 21: 1–11	Palm Sunday transport	Descriptive style
Luke 9: 1–6	Instructions for the twelve apostles	Achievement style
John 21: 11–18	Recommissioning of Peter	Personal style
John 6: 1–15	Feeding the five thousand	Democratic style
John 13: 1–17	Washing the disciples' feet	Pace-setting style
Mark 9: 14–29	Deliverance of the boy with a demon	Mentoring style

Devised by Rick Warren: see *The Purpose-Driven Life* (Zondervan, 2002)

Reflection on learning

What SHAPE* are you?

> **You will need:**
> * A flip chart
> * Paper and pen for each participant

Write the letters of the word SHAPE down the page on the flip chart and introduce the acronym, briefly explaining each part of it:

- Spiritual gifts: how are you gifted?
- Heart: what are you passionate about?
- Abilities: what skills do you have and what can you do?
- Personality: how do you come across to other people?
- Experience: what experiences can you draw upon in your work with children?

Invite each participant to think about their unique SHAPE and to write down something under each heading that will help them in their work with children. For each part of the acronym, ask a few people to feed back some things they are happy to share from what they have written. Draw out the point that each person's SHAPE is unique, God-given and valuable.

> **Trainer's note**
> This activity is closely linked with one of the acts of worship below ('God-given SHAPE') and could be done as part of it.

What would you do if…?

> **You will need:**
> * Copies of the 'What would you do if…?' scenarios (p. 118)

Divide into small groups and give each group one of the scenarios as follows.

- You've had a bad day at school, you're in a bad mood and one of the children in the group is behaving in a way that annoys you. You're getting more and more wound up. What do you do?
- You get an email or phone message asking you to prepare something for the children's group, but you know you won't be available. What do you do?

❧ You are asked to tell a particular Bible story at the children's club in two weeks' time, but you haven't even heard of the story before and don't know where it is in the Bible. What do you do?

❧ A child asks you to give her a piggyback or hold him by the arms and swing him round and round. How do you respond?

❧ A child is sitting alone and looking upset. He or she seems reluctant to join in the activity with the other children. You are not involved in leading the activity. What do you do?

❧ An adult leader seems to be struggling to tell a story because a small number of children keep calling out and making silly noises. You are sitting with the children and you feel bored with the story yourself. What do you do?

❧ You have been asked to pick the 'Star of the Week' in the children's club. The child who seemed to behave the best has often been given this award and, as usual, is sitting quietly and waiting patiently. Another child is eagerly saying 'Me, me, me' and stretching his hand in the air. You know he has been trying really hard today, even though his behaviour is often quite difficult to manage. What do you do?

❧ During a small group discussion about the Bible story that the children have just heard, one of them asks a question to which you don't know the answer. How do you respond?

Ask each small group to discuss what they would do as young leaders in that situation and role-play it together. Then, invite each small group to act out their role-play in front of everyone else.

You may wish to relate this activity back to the different styles of leadership discussed in the 'Biblical thought'.

What's wrong? _____

> **You will need:**
> ✳ An adult translation of the Bible and a children's translation (such as the *International Children's Bible*)

The trainer role-plays some of the following scenarios, with the participants acting the part of a group of children. Build in the examples of bad practice listed for each scenario.

After each role-play, ask what was not helpful for children and how the scenario could have been done better. Then invite someone to role-play the situation in a better way.

❧ Leading a game with a group of children: Talk to the group while looking at the floor; start explaining the rules but then break off, saying, 'I'm sure you all know the rules anyway'; say something like 'I hope you'll play better than you did last week, because you were rubbish.'

❧ Telling a short story: Start by telling the children 'I'm going to tell you a story, the one where Jesus heals a man who was paralysed.' Read Luke 5:17–26 straight from an adult translation of the Bible, in a monotone voice without any expression, and hide your face behind the book.

❧ Leading a discussion with a group of children about the story used in the previous scenario: Start by using only closed questions with 'yes' or 'no' answers, such as 'Was the man in the story paralysed?', 'Did his friends bring him to Jesus?' and so on. Invite answers from the same one or two people in the group, ignoring the rest. Ask a more open question—for example, 'How did the man feel in this story?' Then, when someone offers an obvious answer, such as 'The man felt sad because he couldn't walk' or 'The man felt happy because he could walk again', respond with a put-down—for example, 'Of course the man felt sad, that's obvious. Can't you do better than that?'

Worship

DIY worship _____

> **You will need:**
> ✳ A selection of resources (see p. 110)

Ask the group to create an act of worship together. Give the participants a theme which has arisen from the training session, such as 'servanthood' or 'one body, many parts'. Split them into small groups and ask each group to choose a focus, such as music, prayer, drama, creating a sacred space, artwork, Bible reading, thought for the day, coordination and so on.

Provide a selection of resources that could be useful in an act of worship. Give the groups time to look at the resources and decide what they want to use and how they can use it so that each group member plays a part. Encourage interaction between the groups as they create the act of worship. (The coordinator or coordination group will need to facilitate this interaction.) Then bring the groups together and use the form of worship that has been created. The aim is to involve every member of each group in worship.

Resource ideas

- Bibles; meditations or books on prayer; poetry books
- CDs or MP3s with a selection of worship music
- CD player or MP3 player and speakers
- Laptop and projector
- Glue
- Music books
- Fabric
- Instruments
- Stones
- Wallpaper lining roll
- Bowls
- Art materials
- Water
- Paper
- Oils
- Post-it notes
- Maps or globe
- Pens
- Pictures or photos
- Clay
- Magazines and newspapers
- Candles
- Scissors

Sent to serve: a meditative reading

Read the following meditation and Bible passage, allowing time for silence in the appropriate places.

'Close your eyes, bow your head, breathe in slowly through your nose, hold your breath for a moment and then let it out. As I read this passage, don't try to think about it; just listen. Feel the rhythm of the words and the power of the text. Don't analyse the words; just experience them.'

Read Isaiah 6:1–8.

Silence

'Now, as I read the text again, listen for words or phrases that jump out to you.'

Read Isaiah 6:1–8.

Silence

'This time, as I read the text, imagine you are there. Try to place yourself in Isaiah's place. Think about how you would respond to the sights and sounds that he describes. Let the words of God, spoken to Isaiah, be spoken to you.'

Read Isaiah 6:1–8.

Silence

Will you serve me?

> **You will need:**
> * Bible
> * Bowls and towels
> * A picture of Jesus washing Peter's feet

Ask volunteers to read each of the following passages.

Reader 1

I am a child living less than a mile from here. I am growing up pretty much on my own. I go to a club at your church. Mum treats me like I'm a nuisance and most people act like I don't even exist. I need someone to look at me, to spend time with me. I need someone to love me for me. Will you listen to me and take the time to know me?

Reader 2

I am old now, or at least that is what you would say. I don't feel old, but I guess I am. I used to have friends and my family to visit me. I used to lead Sunday school. I am lonely. I feel like nothing I do matters. I have lived; I have learned. Will you listen to me, sit with me, learn from me, give me purpose and include me?

Reader 3

I am your neighbour. I live outside your church community. You see me every day and we are polite to each other, always nodding heads or saying 'hello'. I am the person you see in the corridors at school or the quiet person in your class, but you don't know me. Will you be kind to me? Will you take time to know me?

Put out a number of bowls of clean water and towels. Read John 13:1–17 and encourage the group to think about Jesus' actions. Invite participants to respond *either* by washing one another's hands or feet (let them choose) as a sign that they want to follow Jesus' example and be servant leaders, *or* by taking some time to look at and think about a picture of Jesus washing Peter's feet.

Offer a blessing at the end, maybe using the words of John 13:20.

God given SHAPE

> **You will need:**
> * Scissors, pens, glue
> * Copies of the people outline, hexagons or cube net (pp. 119–121)
> * Music

Do one of the creative prayer activities below as a way to give thanks for our God-given SHAPE (Spiritual gifts, Heart, Abilities, Personality, Experience, as explained above).

❖ Cut out people outlines. As an individual, write each aspect of your SHAPE on it, then stick all the outlines together on a large piece of card to create a team.
❖ Write your name and the five aspects of your SHAPE around the six edges of a hexagon, then stick the hexagons together on a large piece of card to form a tessellating pattern.
❖ Make small gift boxes and write on the six faces of the cube your name and the five aspects of your SHAPE.

Offer these creative expressions of each person's God-given SHAPE back to God, perhaps with appropriate background music. Provide time to pray silently or aloud.

River of gifts

You will need:
✳ Wallpaper lining roll
✳ Post-it notes
✳ Pens

Lay the wallpaper out along the floor. Draw a river on it running from one end to the other. Hand out Post-it notes to the group and ask them to explore, in pairs, their unique sets of gifts. Write each gift on a Post-it note and stick it on the river. The group can then spend some time looking at all the gifts on the river. After this, say a closing prayer, such as the one below, thanking God and acknowledging all the gifts flowing on the river.

Loving God, you created us as part of your world and sustain us with the waters of your love. Help us to be proud of the gifts you have given us, letting them fill our lives and flow through us to bring your love to the children we meet. Amen

Song suggestions
You may wish to sing an appropriate worship song. Talk to the young people to find songs that are meaningful to them and/or look at a relevant website. For music samples and reviews to give you ideas, visit:
www.crossrhythms.co.uk

Advert for a children's worker

Design a simple job advertisement for a children's worker

Name of advertiser
Title of position
Time commitment required
A brief description of the role
The main skills required
Contact details

Outline of a child

What's their favourite game?
What makes them laugh?
Can they read yet?
Who do they live with?
Are they quiet or loud?
What do they most enjoy doing?

Common characteristics of children aged 3–5 years

(Taken from *Art of 3s–11s*, Rachel Heathfield and Simon Marshall, SU, 1997)

Has little sense of right or wrong

Obeys rules to receive rewards

Imitates others

Asks questions to learn

Confuses the real and imaginary

Learns best from physical activities

Recalls events

Responds to the hero in the story

Self-centred

Plays alongside rather than with others

Respects grown-ups

Invents

Experiences awe and wonder

Asks 'why?'

Takes stories and symbols literally

Reproduced with permission from *More Core Skills for Children's Work* published by BRF 2010 (978 1 84101 700 6) www.barnabasinchurches.org.uk

Common characteristics of children aged 5–7 years

(Taken from *Art of 3s–11s*, Rachel Heathfield and Simon Marshall, SU, 1997)

Wants to please

Avoids blame and guilt

Obeys rules to receive rewards

Asks questions to learn

Adds, subtracts and reads

Learns best from physical activities

Classifies, relates and orders

Recalls events

Enjoys being part of an organised group

Eager to be accepted by children of the same age group

Experiences awe and wonder

Respects grown-ups

Hand–eye coordination improves

Runs, jumps and skips

Imitates adult faith

Responds to the hero in a story

Reproduced with permission from *More Core Skills for Children's Work* published by BRF 2010 (978 1 84101 700 6) www.barnabasinchurches.org.uk

Common characteristics of children aged 7–11 years

(Taken from *Art of 3s–11s*, Rachel Heathfield and Simon Marshall, SU, 1997)

Avoids blame and guilt

Sees fairness as vital

Adds, subtracts and reads

Fantasy becomes less important

Enjoys being part of an organised group

Eager to be accepted by children of the same age group

Has finer coordination

Is restless when still

Is conscious of appearance

Imitates adult faith

May experience a vivid relationship with God

Descriptive style

The 'Do it the way I tell you' leader who closely controls people. (Although this sounds harsh, it may sometimes be the most appropriate style for a situation.)

Democratic style

The 'One person, one vote' leader who encourages people's input in decision-making and recognises and rewards team effort.

Achievement style

The 'Firm but fair' leader who gives people clear direction and encourages by persuasion and feedback on task performance.

Pace-setting style

The 'Do it myself' leader who performs many tasks personally, expects members to follow his or her example and challenges by setting high standards and letting people work on their own.

Personal style

The 'People first, task second' leader who emphasises personal relationships in the organisation and stimulates people by trying to keep them happy with fringe benefits, security, social activities and a comfortable atmosphere.

Mentor style

The 'You can do it' leader who helps and encourages members to improve their performance, and encourages by providing opportunities for personal development.

Reproduced with permission from *More Core Skills for Children's Work* published by BRF 2010 (978 1 84101 700 6) www.barnabasinchurches.org.uk

'What would you do if...?' scenarios

You've had a bad day at school, you're in a bad mood and one of the children in the group is behaving in a way that annoys you. You're getting more and more wound up. What do you do?

A child is sitting alone and looking upset. He or she seems reluctant to join in the activity with the other children. You are not involved in leading the activity. What do you do?

You get an email or phone message asking you to prepare something for the children's group, but you know you won't be available. What do you do?

An adult leader seems to be struggling to tell a story because a small number of children keep calling out and making silly noises. You are sitting with the children and you feel bored with the story yourself. What do you do?

You are asked to tell a particular Bible story at the children's club in two weeks' time, but you haven't even heard of the story before and don't know where it is in the Bible. What do you do?

You have been asked to pick the 'Star of the Week' in the children's club. The child who seemed to behave the best has often been given this award and, as usual, is sitting quietly and waiting patiently. Another child is eagerly saying 'Me, me, me' and stretching his hand in the air. You know he has been trying really hard today, even though his behaviour is often quite difficult to manage. What do you do?

A child asks you to give her a piggyback or hold him by the arms and swing him round and round. How do you respond?

During a small group discussion about the Bible story that the children have just heard, one of them asks a question to which you don't know the answer. How do you respond?

Reproduced with permission from *More Core Skills for Children's Work* published by BRF 2010 (978 1 84101 700 6) www.barnabasinchurches.org.uk

People outline

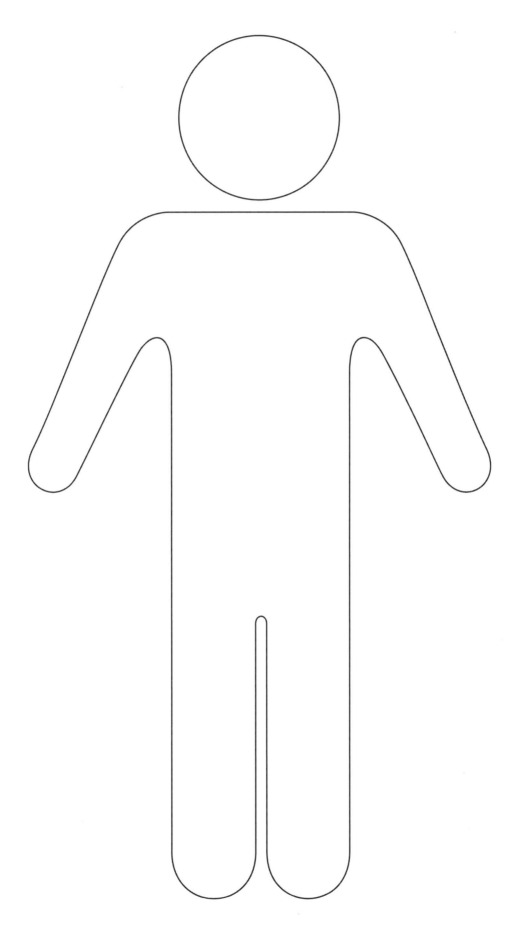

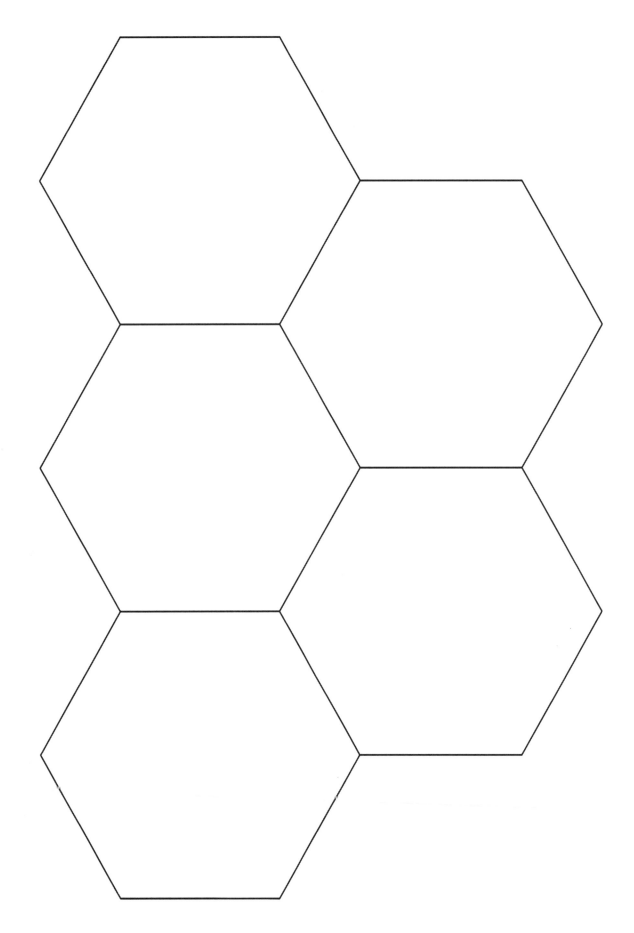

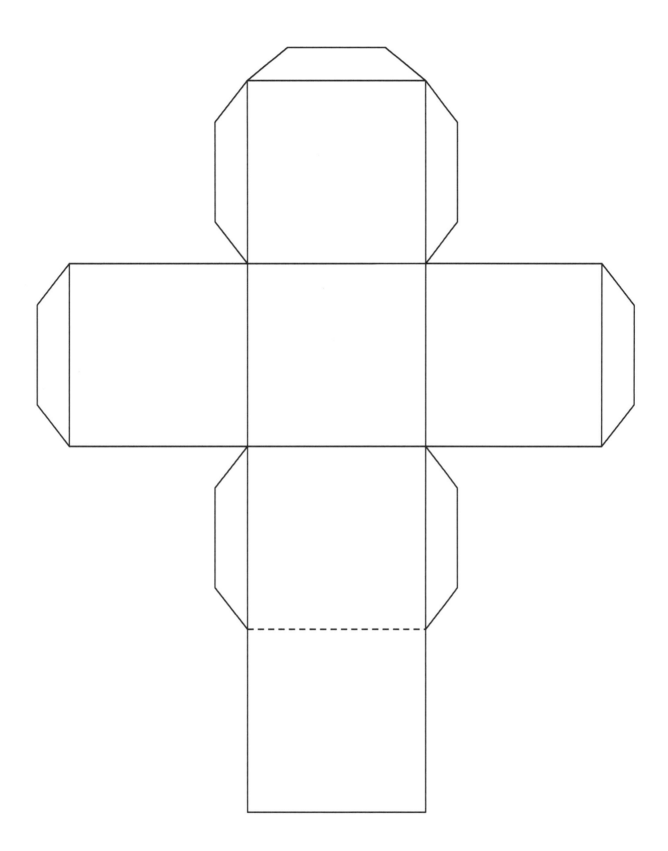

Top tips for leading games

✤ Prepare as much as possible beforehand. Make sure you know the rules and how to explain them clearly. (Try writing them out if you have never led this game before.) Make sure all the equipment needed is available.

✤ Wait until the children are sitting down quietly and looking at you before you start introducing the game. Counting down from 5 to 0 is a good way to encourage the children to finish their conversations and be quiet. Don't talk over them. Make sure they are quiet before you continue.

✤ Don't assume that everyone knows how to play the game, even if they say they do. (Many popular games have a wide range of rules, depending on who you ask!) Explain the aim and rules of the game and clearly say where the children need to be at the start of the game—for example, 'Everyone sit in a circle around me' or 'Team 1, sit in a straight line behind George; Team 2, sit in a line behind Mary.'

✤ Divide the children into teams if necessary. Try to create equal teams by looking for pairs of children who are similar in ability and putting one in each team. Alternatively, do it randomly by numbering each child from one to four and then asking all the number ones to get together, all the twos, all the threes, and all the fours. It's best to avoid choosing team captains and allowing children to pick their own teams, as this usually leaves a few children feeling unwanted. It's also best to avoid setting boys against girls. If you can, assign a leader to look after each team.

✤ If it's a new game for many of the children, demonstrate how the game goes (perhaps asking one or two of the children to help you).

✤ If someone makes a mistake very early in the game and it's clear that they have misunderstood the rules, stop the game, say that it was a 'practice', quickly explain the relevant rules and start again.

✤ Give out the equipment to each team only when you have finished explaining and demonstrating the game.

✤ During the game, try to be fair and firm. The referee's decision is final. Let other leaders deal with any individual children's needs during the game. Don't let individual children distract you from managing the game.

✤ Encourage and praise children during the game. When the game is finished, praise the children if they've played well or fairly or tried hard.

✤ If it is a competitive game, announce the results from the bottom team upwards, but say (for example) 'fourth' rather than 'last'. Encourage the children to praise each other by clapping each team in turn as they are mentioned.

✤ Finally, hand over to another leader for the next activity with a clear instruction, such as 'Now everyone sit down and listen to Emily.'

✤ Choose carefully which games to play. Try to fit the game with the theme of the session in some way. Ensure that the game reflects the ethos and values you want to promote in your group.

✤ Avoid competitive games whenever possible: a cooperative ethos is best for learning.

Top tips for storytelling

✤ Be prepared. Know your story—not word for word, but know the setting, the characters, the direction the story is taking or the important events.

✤ Use expression—different voices for different characters or emotions. Speak at different speeds depending on the events, and use different volumes, from a whisper to a shout.

✤ Use repetition—of a key phrase, a key line or a key question in the story.

✤ Use space and movement. Organise your hearers to create a sense of space and move around to reflect movement within the story.

✤ Use visual aids—for example, pictures, faces, puppets, or a story box with objects that, one by one, help you to tell the story.

✤ Use mystery. Leave loose ends that will prompt questions and further imagination. Perhaps even ask, 'What do you think happened next?'

Reproduced with permission from *More Core Skills for Children's Work* published by BRF 2010 (978 1 84101 700 6) www.barnabasinchurches.org.uk

✤ Use interaction—hearers joining in with a key phrase, actions for key words within the story, sound effects and so on.
✤ Use different perspectives. Tell the story from the perspective of different characters within the story.
✤ Use variety. Choose different types of story and different styles of telling each time.

Top tips for leading a discussion

✤ Preparation is important. Think about the topic for discussion beforehand. If there is to be discussion of a Bible reading or a story, make sure you know it well. Prepare some questions that will help to get people thinking and talking about it.
✤ Seat the group in a way that allows everyone to see one another (for example, in a circle or semi-circle).
✤ Provide paper and pencil or a flip chart for your co-leader or someone else to jot down the main points that arise. Later in the discussion, you may wish to refer back to these points.
✤ Don't let the discussion go on too long. Start and end on time. Remember that young children will find it difficult to sit still and concentrate for a long time.
✤ Encourage a relaxed atmosphere by starting with an icebreaker question and giving every member of the group a chance to answer—for example, 'If you could be a sweet, what kind of sweet would you be?' and so on.
✤ Set ground rules that help everyone to participate, such as:
  • When someone is talking, everyone else should listen.
  • If you have something to say, don't just interrupt but put your hand up and wait patiently.
  • Only the person holding the beanbag, shell (or similar) is allowed to talk.
  • Talk to each other rather than shouting at each other.
  • Don't say things that put someone else down.
✤ Start off with one or two simple factual questions—for example, 'Who are the main characters in this story?', 'What job did Zacchaeus do?' and so on.
✤ Try to ask open questions that don't have one right answer—for example, 'Why do you think Jesus chose to speak to Zacchaeus?' or 'How do you think Zacchaeus felt when Jesus spoke to him?' or 'I wonder what Jesus and Zacchaeus talked about when they were having dinner together?'
✤ Affirm each person's contribution and thank them by name.
✤ If someone says something that is unclear, ask questions to encourage the person to explain what they mean. Use an open question like, 'Could you tell us some more about it?'
✤ If someone says something that is factually incorrect, direct the person concerned back to the source to check—for example, 'I'm not sure if Zacchaeus was actually a taxi driver. Could someone look in the Bible and check?'
✤ Encourage answers from individuals who seem ready to talk rather than simply going around the circle in order.
✤ Encourage everyone to contribute. Ask questions to quieter members of the group by name, and invite (but don't force) an answer.
✤ Don't allow anyone to dominate the discussion. Tactfully lead on to another person—for example, 'Thanks for that point, Ruth. Now I wonder what other people think about this?'
✤ Disagreements will be inevitable and should be accepted as normal. Try to defuse a discussion that is becoming a heated argument.
✤ The leader should play an active part in the discussion in order to keep it moving, interesting and focused. Beware, though, of taking over and dominating the discussion.
✤ Try to keep the discussion on track. If it moves in an unhelpful direction, bring it back to the appropriate topic.
✤ During a longer discussion with older children, stop occasionally to review the points that have been made so far.
✤ At the end of the discussion, briefly summarise the main points from the group or ask members of the group to do this themselves.
✤ Consider reporting the group's main points in some way occasionally—for example, to the other children, the congregation or the newsletter editor.

Reproduced with permission from *More Core Skills for Children's Work* published by BRF 2010 (978 1 84101 700 6) www.barnabasinchurches.org.uk

Top tips for leading an act of worship

The aim of worship is to celebrate, reflect, proclaim and pray as a community conscious of the presence of God. It can lead to a fresh awareness of who God is, what God has done and how his actions affect our past, present and future.

✣ Take time to prepare to lead an act of worship.

✣ Meet with anyone who will be leading worship with you, to pray and plan together.

✣ Decide on a theme or topic.

✣ Study the Bible text, pray and prepare the message or teaching.

✣ Worship is intentional and purposeful, and involves the mind, the heart, the body with all its senses, and the soul. Try to include items that deliberately involve the whole person in worship.

✣ Think about how you will encourage people to participate in worship. Who could help in some way? How will all those present be enabled to participate?

✣ Think about what approach to prayer you will use—for example, creative, reflective, liturgical and so on.

✣ Use music that complements the message, and be sensitive to the lyrics. Different people relate to different styles of lyric as well as different styles of music.

✣ Be creative and imaginative in creating a worship space that will complement other aspects.

✣ Prepare in advance any material, props, drama and so on that you need.

✣ Try to create the right atmosphere before the worship begins.

✣ During the act of worship, be sensitive to God's leading and to the group's response, and be flexible in the light of these elements.

✣ Allow space for people to opt out if they are uncomfortable with something.

✣ Stick to the allotted time.

Reproduced with permission from *More Core Skills for Children's Work* published by BRF 2010 (978 1 84101 700 6) **www.barnabasinchurches.org.uk**

Useful resources

Jan Dyer, *100 Prayer Ideas for Children* (Kingsway, 1999)

Lucy Moore, *The Gospels Unplugged* (Barmabas, 2002)

Jonny Baker et al., *Alternative Worship* (SPCK, 2003)

Heather Butler, *35 Stories to Make You Think* (Barnabas, 2008)

Roots for Worship Leaders and *Roots for Children and Young People* (www.rootsontheweb.com)

www.godlyplay.org.uk

Reproduced with permission from *More Core Skills for Children's Work* published by BRF 2010 (978 1 84101 700 6) www.barnabasinchurches.org.uk

Notes

Notes

Bibliography

A Good Childhood, Richard Layard & Judy Dunn (Penguin, 2009)

All God's Children, Marian Carter (SPCK, 2007)

Charter for Children in the Church (URC, 2004)

Children and Bereavement, Wendy Duffy (CHP, 2003)

Chidlren and our Global Future, Kristin Herzog (The Pilgrim Press, 2005)

Dangerous Wonder, Michael Yaconelli (NavPress, 1998)

For Every Child: the rights of a child in words and pictures (Red Fox, 2000)

From the Ground Up: understanding the spiritual world of the child, Kathryn Copsey (Barnabas, 2005)

Good as New: a radical retelling of the Scriptures, John Henson (O Books, 2004)

Grief in Children, Atle Dyregrov (JKP, 2008)

Honouring Children, Kathleen Marshall & Paul Parvis (St Andrews Press, 2004)

Leadership Essentials for Children's Ministry, Craig Jutila (Group Publishing, 2002)

Offering the Gospel to Children, Gretchen Wolff Pritchard (Cowley, 1992)

Special Children Special Needs, Simon Bass (CHP, 2003)

Teaching Godly Play, Jerome Berryman (Morehouse Education Resources, 2009)

The Child in Christian Thought, Marcia Bunge (Eerdmans, 2001)

The Child in the Bible, ed. Marcia Bunge (Eerdmans, 2008)

The Growth of Love, Keith J. White (Barnabas, 2008)

The Spirit of the Child, David Hay & Rebecca Nye (Jessica Kingsley Publishers, 2006)

Through the Eyes of a Child, eds. Anne Richards & Peter Privett, (CHP, 2009)

Top Tips on Handling Difficult Behaviour, Graham Finch (SU, 2005)

Top Tips on Welcoming Special Children, Denise Abrahall (SU, 2005)

Urban Hope and Spiritual Health, Leslie Francis (Epworth, 2006)

Weaving a Just Future for Children, Diane C. Olson & Laura Dean Friedich (Discipleship Resources, 2008)

Where Are the Children?, Margaret Withers (Barnabas, 2005)

Wholly Worship Too (URC, 2000)

Working with 11–14s, Tricia Williams & John Stephenson (SU, 2005)

Working with 8–10s, Claire Saunders and Hilary Porritt (SU, 2005)

Working with Under 5s, Judith Wigley (SU, 2005)